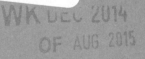

SET *with* STYLE

Caroline Clifton-Mogg

SET *with* STYLE

Photography by Simon Upton

Clarkson Potter/Publishers
New York

There are few things more enjoyable than sitting congenially and comfortably round a table, drinking and eating something delicious in the company of amusing and interesting people. To congenial tables everywhere!

Published in the United States by
Clarkson Potter/Publishers,
an imprint of the Crown Publishing Group,
a division of Random House, Inc., New York.
www.crownpublishing.com
www.clarksonpotter.com

Originally published in slightly different form in Great
Britain by Jacqui Small LLP, an imprint of Aurum Press,
Ltd., London.

Clarkson N. Potter is a trademark and Potter and colophon
are registered trademarks of Random House, Inc.

Library of Congress Cataloging-in-Publication Data is
available upon request

ISBN 978-0-307-39555-9

Printed in China

10 9 8 7 6 5 4 3 2 1

First American Edition

contents

introduction

SHARING FOOD is a natural act of generosity, and it is also natural to want to make the background for the food—the table and its setting—as welcoming and as interesting as possible. And this is something that you do all the time—probably every day of your life.

You may find it a surprising thought, but everyone is capable of setting a great table—it is something that comes naturally—even if you don't always realize it. Every time that you set the table, even for a seemingly routine meal like a weekend breakfast or a kitchen supper, you instinctively make style choices as you go along. You may pick the blue mats rather than the checked ones, because they go well with the white china; or the antique candlesticks because they look pretty with the old crystal glasses you want to use. Or because the red cloth is already on the table, you instinctively get out the green pottery plates from the cupboard. Every day your individual style is evident; sometimes all that we need to do is to refine that style, to draw in some creative new ideas and inspiration and translate them to our own table schemes.

This is where *Set with Style* comes in. Creating a table setting, no matter how simple or instinctive, is actually a—albeit extremely enjoyable—form of interior decoration, so for this book, we have asked international designers and decorators—people who are incredibly creative in their own right—to design new tables for us, suitable for all occasions, from the very informal to the celebratory and festive. I look at a number of decorating styles, from the French rural look to the traditional and antique, taking in Oriental style, contemporary and modern along the way, and we have photographed schemes from everything from breakfasts to birthdays.

What I learned from the clever people that I talked to and we photographed is that the most creative and imaginative among us have a talent for choosing and combining the basic elements of any table—the china and glass, the cutlery and linen—and turning them into an inspirational whole; and I also learned an even more important fact—that creating a fabulous table is not a matter of money or even having cupboards bulging with china and glass; it is far more a question of thought and care, because those two qualities produce a welcoming, hospitable and generous table, and that is the best that you could offer any guest.

BELOW A table of contrasts: Rumi Verjee of Thomas Goode has combined luxuriously gilded china, silver water goblets, and an antique golden candelabra with one of a set of artist-designed table mats and an almost volcanic vase.

setting the table

LEFT There is real beauty to appreciate in a table dressed in traditional manner with every detail carefully considered, including such simple individual single-stem flower arrangements.
OPPOSITE The allure of a well-dressed and luxurious table is timeless. Since the 18th century the informal dinner, taken at a round table, lit by candles, dressed with care, and with wine and food set close to hand, has been a quintessential part of good living.
PREVIOUS PAGES As with all the best tables, there is an inherent generosity and promise of good things to come in the table prepared by Tricia Foley in the studio of her Long Island house.

the history of dining

By the Middle Ages, in any large European household, communal eating was not only an accepted part of daily life, but a vitally important one, clarifying and reinforcing, on a regular basis, the relationship between the lord and his household. In such houses, there would be, in the Great Hall, either one long table or, depending on the importance and wealth of the host, two tables—a high table for the most important members of the household and another lower table below it for all other diners.

The meal usually consisted of roast meat and some smaller dishes, and food was taken with the hand, the pieces of meat having usually been cut off with the diner's own knife. The food was eaten from slabs, or trenchers, of bread, which evolved over the succeeding centuries into dishes of wood and later, pewter. The spoon, which evolved from a bowl attached to a handle, was often used in conjunction with both the knife and hands. The fork is a comparative newcomer to the dining table, having made brief appearances throughout the centuries and been dismissed as a merely frivolous utensil. It was not until the

17th century that a three-tined fork was widely used, which eventually became the four-tined fork we use today.

By the 18th century, for feasts and banquets—the menus of which are always more interesting than the everyday food of the time—food was served in almost as much abundance as it had been in Ancient Rome, over 2000 years ago. Service *à la française* was the most popular way of presenting and serving dinner. On entering the dining room the diners would be greeted by the sight of a table not only laid with candelabra, salts and decorative ornaments, but also groaning with food. This was presented in the form of central set pieces, artistically arranged and surrounded by smaller dishes as well as various hors d'oeuvres—literally "outside the main works"—which edged the table. The first course might include soup, meats and then entrées; very often, after this introductory course came the next wave of food—the *really* large dishes—roasted meats and *plats composés*, accompanied by salads, vegetables and even jellies and ices. Not that the jellies constituted dessert. The dessert course—a selection of elaborate confections—was served

separately. Guests were not, as is sometimes mistakenly supposed, expected to eat every dish that had been prepared, but to choose from the dishes within their immediate vicinity, rather than continually asking a servant to bring them tidbits from the far side of the table.

During the 1830's a new, modern way of serving dinner—service *à la russe*—became fashionable. Instead of the dishes being displayed in all their glory on the table, each course was served separately and handed round to the seated diners—in much the same way that we eat today.

One effect of this new form of service was that since the food was handed around, there was more empty space on the table which, during the latter part of the 19th century, began to be filled with more and more extravagant floral decorations, which straddled the length of the table like horticultural colossi. Such tables must have been an amazing sight and although we may prefer our rather simpler settings, which in these do-it-yourself days are a practical necessity as well as an aesthetic choice, it is fascinating to see from what rich beginnings our own three-course dinner is derived.

OPPOSITE Around an antique table with matching dark wood chairs a table has been set that continues the tradition of convivial dining but with a witty decorative twist—as witnessed in the dark brown earthenware dishes and the collection of shell-related objects that fill the center of the table.

RIGHT This smoothly polished wooden table has been set with a combination of old and new—antique Irish cut glass, modern blue and white china with a traditional pattern and intricately embossed scallop-edged white mats.

etiquette and table manners

In civilized society, table manners and etiquette in general have always been important and as early as the medieval period, tracts were being written on such matters. Most societies, both Eastern and Western, agree on the importance of personal cleanliness and the need for consideration for your neighbor. But there have been moments in history when a general concern for civilized behavior has evolved into what could be considered an obsession, as famously epitomized at Louis XIV's court at the palace of Versailles, where the code of etiquette was so elaborate that a man might be ostracized for failing to observe the finer, often inexplicable, details of each social situation.

One aspect of table manners that has always been important, in almost every society and every period, has been on the subject of when it is permissible to use your hands to eat. In British society, for example, asparagus and globe artichokes are considered vegetables that can—indeed should—be eaten with the fingers, while, let's say, leeks or carrots should not. There is a logic here, based on tradition but also what is practically easier, but it is not always immediately transparent to the interested observer.

A phrase sometimes used in describing the placement at a large, formal dinner is to say that someone was seated "below the salt." In rich medieval households, the "salt" was actually a salter (the word cellar comes from the French word *sel* for salt)—a large and often very elaborate vessel wrought in silver or sometimes even gold, which held the precious and expensive condiment. The great and good were seated above this dish, while those deemed to be of less importance sat beyond it.

Not only placement but also the actual dining seats themselves were once subject to rules of etiquette. The Ancient Greeks and Romans reclined on couches rather than chairs at their elaborate and lengthy feasts. It was deemed important, even vital, that each diner faced the same direction, leaning on his left elbow—even though he might be left handed—so that both conversation and food might flow smoothly in a single, harmonious direction. Later, from the medieval period on, the nobility often sat on chairs beneath canopies to denote their elevated status, like the old earl in William Hogarth's series "Marriage à la Mode." A version of this mark of rank was to be seen in Louis XIV's Versailles, where only the king could sit on a chair with arms, while some others, by virtue of their rank, were accorded the privilege of being able to sit on stools. The remnants of this seated one-up-manship remain with us today in the form of a traditional set of dining chairs which includes two "carvers," chairs with arm rests, usually reserved for the host and hostess and perhaps perceived as superior to the other armless chairs in the set.

cultural differences

The cultural differences and variations in the table manners of other societies and groups can often seem illogical, but it is intrinsic to having good manners to be aware of their existence. Although table manners may differ hugely in the particular, they are remarkably similar in the broader picture: in every society, on the whole, cleanliness is preferred to slovenly appearance and behavior, and there is a general consensus about the importance of a show of generosity and hospitality towards the guest.

Knives, for example—in every culture perceived at one level as objects of suppressed violence—are laid in the West with the blades facing in towards the plate—a holdover from the time when they were sharp hunting knives that could possibly have been used in an attack. For the same reason, at the end of the course the knife is laid at rest in the centre of the plate, so that it faces away from a neighbor and is not seen as a threat.

While in Europe a knife and fork are used together to cut and eat, American diners use only a knife to cut the food, laying it to the side of the plate while the fork is then used to actually eat the pieces of food. Actually many societies feel that utensils such as forks are not only cumbersome, but also rather unhygienic, and prefer, as they do in India, to eat with their hands, or more

BELOW LEFT A modern international look can borrow from many different cultures—this tableware was designed by John Pawson with a double-deal plate that can be used both upside down and right side up, and a knife that rests on its handle, blade pointing down.
BELOW RIGHT This table with a highly sophisticated feel has plates of an abstract design designed for Coach by Reed Krakoff, paired with classical cutlery from Puiforcat and glasses by Baccarat for a European feel.

BELOW LEFT A new
concept in ceramics: this set
of dishes designed by
Voon Wong, which can be
interchanged and used for
everything from seasonings
to side dishes, has obvious
Eastern influences and
dining applications.
BELOW RIGHT Simple yet
not; a conglomeration of
styles and periods, cultures
and colors with a clever
Oriental twist seen in the
napkins circled with Indian
bracelets and the elaborate
inlaid dining chairs.

usually with one hand, which is always the right one, even if you are naturally left-handed. Similarly, in countries where chopsticks are used, such as China and Japan, the sticks should always be used in the right hand. And they should never be left stuck upright in a bowl of rice, as this resembles the position of incense sticks, which are customarily left as an offering to the dead.

The number of diners around a table, both in our own society and others, can be a matter of discussion; in many societies, the number thirteen is considered unlucky and should the diners reach that number, a doll or stuffed animal will often be placed in an empty chair to bring the numbers up to fourteen.

Not that all cultures sit around a communal table—in many countries, the diner sits on the floor to eat from trays, while others—like the Ancient Greeks were wont to do—have small individual tables set in front of them. Chinese tables are round or square, rather than oval or oblong as we prefer in the West, while, as previously discussed, in Ancient Greek and Roman society, men ate reclining on couches—a posture that must have needed a great deal of practice before comfort was achieved.

Of course there are obviously many other differences between the eating habits of different cultures, or even different groups within societies, but few that consideration and concern for the feelings of your hosts will not overcome!

how to lay a place setting

The accepted way to lay a place setting in Britain is derived from that of the formal banquet, albeit—unsurprisingly in the 21st century—somewhat simpler. The guiding principle is extremely logical: on either side of the plate, the cutlery is set in the order in which you will use it, working from the outside in, with the knives to the right of the plate and the forks to the left. So, for a formal dinner of soup, a main course and dessert, the soup spoon is the outer utensil, followed by a dinner knife, the blade facing inwards, with, next to the plate, the dessert spoon. To the left of the plate will be a dinner fork on the outside and a smaller, dessert fork placed next to the plate. Both are laid with the tines facing upwards.

If the first course is not soup but an hors d'oeuvre, then a small knife would be substituted for the soup spoon, and a small fork laid outside the dinner fork. In this case, to avoid seemingly never ending lines of cutlery stretching into infinity, the dessert spoon and fork might be laid above the plate, with the spoon on top, its bowl pointing to the left, and the fork below it, pointing in the opposite direction. If a bread knife is used, it would be laid across the side plate. Glasses are laid to the right of the plate, again roughly in the order in which you use them, with the water glass close at hand, the smaller white wine glass behind or beside that, and the larger red wine glass behind.

For an everyday meal, where the same cutlery is used for more than one course, the knife and fork are laid either side of the plate with the dessert spoon and fork on top.

An American setting is very similar to a British one, other than that fish knives and forks are sometimes used for formal dinners and are therefore set on either side of the plate in the correct position for the fish course, depending on whether fish is served as the first or the main course.

For a formal French dinner, the forks are laid in the same way as at a British dinner, but with the tines facing downwards and spoons set with their bowls facing the table. Sometimes a knife rest is used, so that the knife can be retained for other courses. The French do not serve butter with bread, so no side plate is laid, and no bread knife. When setting an Asian meal, particularly Chinese, the chopsticks are laid to the right of the plate, on a chopstick rest. A rice bowl is positioned behind the plate to the left, with a tea bowl and a small dish for sauces to the right.

A Japanese setting will depend very much on the food to be served, the occasion and even the season often being taken into account in traditional Japanese cookery, where texture, shape and color are as important as the food served. The basic requirements however are a rice bowl on the left of the setting and a lidded soup bowl on the right. A beaker for tea is positioned behind the soup dish, as is a sauce dish.

ABOVE LEFT Eastern in a Western way: cultures and styles can be combined in a way that is both easy and attractive. Those elements unique to an Asian table, such as the chopsticks and rice and sauce bowls, all have their customary and expected positions.

ABOVE RIGHT Styles and periods can be combined in a formal place setting; what is important is that the diner has everything easily at hand. Precision is also a key element in producing a pleasing result: note the sharp alignment of the cutlery placement.

TOP LEFT More and more of us eat many of our meals in the living room, or a combined multifunction space, where the table is an integral part of the overall scheme and the setting should always blend with the style of the room as a whole.
ABOVE LEFT During hot weather or in hotter climates, a roof terrace is the ideal place to eat. This terrace in France faces directly south so some shade is needed from the fierce sun for comfortable dining in the middle of the day. Carolyn Quartermaine's light hand-painted curtains shelter the table from the fiercest rays.

TOP RIGHT What could be nicer than to eat on a terrace overlooking the Atlantic ocean? Vicente Wolf takes breakfast here every morning on small tables arranged for the purpose.
ABOVE RIGHT The kitchen has expanded beyond its traditional role of the place for food preparation and cooking, and has now also become a welcoming place in which to eat. Guests can become more involved in the food preparation process, or at the very least offer good conversation to keep the cook company. But it is important to set an area aside and take as much effort with the setting as you would if the table were in a separate room.

where to eat

Until comparatively recently—even in the latter part of the 20th century—the dining room was viewed as an essential reception room in any house, the room where you ate the main meals of the day. Breakfast might have been eaten in the kitchen, which was usually a working room with often not much more than a small kitchen table, and tea might have been served in the sitting room, but lunch and dinner were invariably dining room meals, with all the attendant formality that that implies.

Slowly though, the dining room became less important, used only when entertaining and on formal, traditional occasions, and as it became less important, the kitchen began to become more so, with the result today that many homes now have a kitchen in which all meals are eaten, with no separate dining room at all. Such a setup is fine, but it does mean that if you do not have one room that is dedicated to eating, then it is more important to devote some thought into making the area where you do eat as pleasant and as welcoming as possible.

Few of the tables photographed in this book are in dedicated dining rooms; some are tables that are set in part of the living room, others are tables that are in part of the kitchen; some tables are in sacrosanct corners; other tables are set up where the whim takes the cook at that moment. Some are in corridors, others in grand drawing rooms. Some of these tables are only used for eating, other tables have another function at other times of the day, and others still are sets of small tables, used separately or together depending on the numbers and the occasion.

So although there are no cut and dried answers to the question, there is a common strand that runs through all these varied solutions, and that is that flexibility and, above all, lateral thinking are the keys to where you eat.

ABOVE RIGHT Although there are not as many formal dining rooms as there once were, those lucky owners of such live up to the high standards expected of them. There is no more perfect backdrop for a grand occasion than a dedicated space.
RIGHT This modern take on informal eating is in Sally Sirkin Lewis' apartment, with zebra-pattern covered chairs set either side of a Lucite table, which has been laid in a formal, but light-hearted manner. A setting for two people such as this can quickly and easily be created in a corner of a room for a relaxed lunch.

table styles

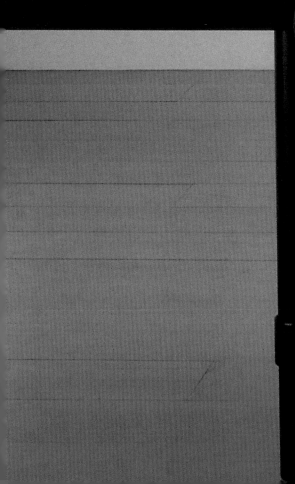

THERE ARE AS MANY WAYS TO SET A TABLE as there are personalities and how we do it depends as much on our background, likes, and dislikes, as on as the way we live. The "correct" way to lay a table developed over centuries, and by the late 18th century, a standardized setting had evolved that included napkin, plate, knife, fork, spoon and goblet for every guest. A century later, the formal version of this—that is to say, as used at a large dinner party or banquet—would have included different sets of knives and forks for fish, fruit, cheese and so on, and a whole range of glasses to cover every drinking eventuality from champagne and water to brandy and sherry. The dinner service itself would have included soup bowls, dinner plates and side plates, as well as dessert plates, and various matching serving dishes; and it is this comprehensive setting that is the basis of our own formal style today— although today's idea of a formal table is generally both easier on the eye and lighter on the table than in the 19th century.

In a sense, all other ways of table setting derive from this template—informal simply means less formal than the traditional and the variants are as many as your imagination will allow, and the occasion demands. One of the joys of living in less constrained times is that there is no one-size-fits-all— the occasion, the venue, the guests, and the menu can help you to decide what flights of fancy you are going to pursue.

OPPOSITE A riot of designs and colors, ranging from English majolica to coloured bendy glasses and a plastic coated floral cloth, are cleverly worked together to make an utterly modern, informal table.
PREVIOUS PAGES Peri Wolfman uses tables on wheels that can easily be brought together to seat a larger number. Her set of Arne Jacobsen chairs was bought in several different, though always neutral, shades so that she can mix them together as desired.

formal

For some people it may be traditional, for others, rather modern
—but there will always be a certain discipline in the way that
the formal table is arranged and the food presented.

LEFT The modern, even minimalist, interior of Rumi Verjee's London house is a plain canvas for the luxury and eclectisism of his grand table arrangements.
THIS PAGE Even when he sets a formal table, Rumi likes an element of contrast. Here he has used lay plates of beaten stainless steel beneath a delicate lidded soup cup by Nymphenburg in a design dating from the 19th century. Contemporary rectangular side dishes by Sawaya Moroni hold blue-and-white checked napkins. Graceful white ceramic swans by Meissen form the centerpiece with a 20th-century silver candelabra.

A WEALTH OF TRADITION
The venerable china store, Thomas Goode, founded in 1827, is known for its sumptuous tables. Rumi Verjee is the present chairman of Thomas Goode and, unsurprisingly, is passionate about tableware.

His contemporary house in London's Notting Hill is the scene for many of his table's extravaganzas. Simple in design and decoration, it is nonetheless formal, and the tables that he creates reflect this. Rumi Verjee loves to entertain and for him the food and the table must complement each other. The look that he espouses is both disciplined—reflecting the design of the house—and rich, a difficult combination to do well. "For me," he says, "A table should be just as much a feast for the eye as it is for the stomach." And to that end, he prefers to serve simple but well-prepared food, against a background of complex and often intricate table design. For Rumi and the designer Goran Svilar, with whom he works closely, nothing is really too over-the-top. Everything has its own beauty, which can be appreciated as long as each aspect of the whole is balanced out—the rich with the simple,

RIGHT A final flourish: the pudding course is served on a set of "Adam and Eve" plates by Fornasettit. These sit on the same beaten steel charger plates used for the first course, and are augmented by gilded port glasses and an elaborate antique set of gold tea and coffee pots and milk jug.

"I like the element of surprise on a table; the changing of the settings throughout the meal."

LEFT For the main course simple, subtly beautiful pierced ware porcelain dinner plates by Hering form a strong contrast with the heavily gilded glasses by Moser and cutlery by Puiforcat. The neutral slate-gray tone of the table surface serves equally well for each and all of the variations placed upon it.

the fragile with the sturdy. "I like to work towards an eclectic balance between the old and the new," a theory he puts into practice by using beautiful French porcelain lidded soup dishes of 19th-century design with uncompromisingly modern, stark white plates, and beaten metal chargers. And surprise is part of his eclecticism. "I like to hold a grand picnic and have present both a butler in a tailcoat and my table designer, Goran Svilar, wearing blue jeans."

Unsurprisingly, Rumi Verjee dislikes mediocrity and loves craftsmanship of any kind; Thomas Goode is justly famous for the quality of its wares and its chairman appreciates equally the beauty of a porcelain Meissen swan, and a sweeping contemporary silver candelabra, both of which, incidentally, he likes to use on the same table. He also likes to mix the simple with the exclusive—table mats made by a contemporary artist in the East End of London, for example, on a table graced with an ornate 18th-century candelabra.

This is something that many creative people do: using the table as a background for diverse and interesting beautiful objects—objects which then become talking points for the diners. He is also keen on changing, subtly, the look of the table as the dinner progresses. "I like the element of surprise on a table; the changing of the settings throughout the meal." Texture is important too—from the surface of the table to the tableware itself. "I might use a beautiful Japanese vessel in earthenware, and then—back to contrast again—put it in front of a piece of reflective silver."

But in the end, as with all good hosts, for him it is ultimately the company which counts. "It is important to me that guests feel comfortable and not too precious. That is the most important thing about a table."

MEDITERRANEAN ELEGANCE French designer Nicolette Schouten can, and does, do formal: it is traditional, but translated into an essentially natural manner.

Her house is so arranged that any number of people can dine in any number of ways: most of the tables are set in the garden or within a stone's throw of a terrace, but in the main body of the house there is a formal dining room where elegantly presented dinners take place. "When we eat in this room, it pleases me to have everything exactly right, with the table set in traditional style; it makes a change, and it is extremely pleasant to be here," says Nicolette.

An 18th-century nobleman would feel quite at home in this room, indeed be happy to dine here—he would enjoy the high-backed upholstered chairs ("always have comfortable chairs," is Nicolette's advice). He would recognize the full richness of the floor-length silk curtains, and he would appreciate the place settings themselves—the porcelain, the silver-handled knives and the pristine white cloth. The chandelier is hung low above the table, and the candles, in silver holders, flicker. At either end of the table, the heads of low-cut flowers nestle in low glass bowls. An unconventional touch, and subtle contrast of color, comes in the lilac glass goblets that echo a tone of the silk curtains.

"When we eat in this room, it pleases me to have everything exactly right, with the table set in traditional style."

BELOW An imaginative and eye-catching flower arrangement does not detract from the abundant pleasures of the table: hydrangeas and Queen Annes lace have been cut down to their heads and massed in shallow, plain cylindrical bowls.

OPPOSITE The large table is set with comfort and elegance; the tones of the table settings—the lilac-tinted glass, the lilac cloth and napkins bordered with lilac, all from Nicolette's design company and shop, Collection Privée in Cannes, are echoed by the antique silver.

ABOVE The setting is a symphony of delicate shades and shapes; silver and glass, with the antique English decorative decanters used as an integral part of the complete table scheme.

contemporary

A contemporary look to a table is one that is not bound by traditional shape or design. It is usually relatively simple and pared down, relying on carefully chosen pieces put together with care.

LEFT This is contemporary table style at its best. Peri Wolfman's take on style seems simple, and is simple, but is so carefully and intelligently worked out. The long table is actually two—a matching pair, and brought together when needed. Peri always uses a limited color palette, and the chairs—there are 20 of them, all Arne Jacobsen's Series 7 design—are in white, black and gray.
RIGHT The china, naturally, is predominantly white, but hints of color are allowed to infiltrate, such as this pale turquoise plate.

CLEAN-CUT MODERNISM Peri Wolfman has long been involved with all that is necessary for the setting of a beautiful table. Formerly head of the tableware product design team at Williams-Sonoma, she is now a product designer and, naturally, specializes in tableware.

Peri Wolfman and husband Charles Gold live in a light-filled contemporary house on Long Island. It is a big change for them—their last house was a period farmhouse and since their move, Peri has looked at interiors—and the table in particular—with a completely fresh eye. "I wanted something that is totally different from the way we lived before and when we first moved in here, it was difficult to put any furniture or objects in it at all—the empty space was so calm! I really value the simple look now—where once I wanted to use as many pieces as possible, now I want to pare down all the time. I think that it is the result of having been in the business for so long, and having

actually been over-stimulated professionally. I still have a lot of things but I find that I just want to keep editing."

The result of this editing shows on the table too. Peri has always liked a limited color palette. "It used to be whites, creams and celadon, and I never, ever had patterned plates. Or patterned napkins for that matter. But now that I'm living here, I like even more sculptural pieces, white, a bit of black, with sometimes just a small bit of extra color"—as in the pale turquoise plates that she has used over the white ones for the first course at her dining table.

Every aspect of dining has been carefully thought out in the new home—first the table, which actually is two separate tables, each 10ft (3m) long and which when put together can seat 20 people. "Usually we keep them apart so that you can walk between them around the room."

And then there is the selection of chairs. "They are stacking chairs designed by Arne Jacobsen—the Series 7. We have twenty altogether and we bought them in three

different shades—white, black and gray, so that when we use them at the table they make a composition in themselves."

The tables are simply laid—a small stack of plates at each setting with the turquoise on top and very simple glasses—although one design is not quite as simple as it seems. "The rounded goblet is actually a Bordeaux glass without a stem, which I designed for Williams-Sonoma." It adds a clever and witty touch to the table.

She likes to use flowers, but only seasonal ones, and not surprisingly, she really doesn't like "multi-colored ones." On that front, she thinks laterally too—sometimes I prefer to use fruit or vegetables as decoration—a pile of yellow peppers or green apples, perhaps." Napkins are large—24in (60cm) square, and were hard to find—lighting is "very, very low, with lots and lots of candles everywhere in the room." Much considered thought has gone into every aspect of the table, and it pays huge dividends—the pleasing result is a clean, cool and, above all, very calm look.

ABOVE A modern table set using a strong monochrome palette means that you can completely change the look of the setting at each course with very little effort:. Here, a square plate is laid as a base for a bowl of berries. RIGHT Napkins in the Wolfman household are always black or white, and must be generously sized.

OPPOSITE The tablemats that Peri prefers are always the same color as the table—black—so as not to stand out too much, circular in shape and slightly larger than the service plate. The tumbler is Peri's own design.

CUTTING-EDGE DESIGN Reed Krakoff is the hugely successful president and creative director of Coach, long associated with classic American design. Under Reed's direction, this once traditional leather company has become achingly chic. He and his wife Delphine live in New York City.

"I want the table to look like an outgrowth of my personal life—not something that has been kept hidden in cupboards."

ABOVE Reed and Delphine Krakoff entertain around a table in the living room of their New York apartment. The wall-to-wall bookshelves provide a comfortable, relaxed background.

OPPOSITE The table, a 20th-century design by Charlotte Perriand, is set with plates designed by Reed for Coach and Baccarat glasses. It is decorated with objects plucked from around the house, and used to great effect on the table.

Reed Krakoff is a man with his finger on the pulse of what is new and happening in all areas of design, and with a fine-tuned ability to translate that into a style that is contemporary and yet not intimidating. He lives design and in his home life as in his work, both he and wife Delphine espouse a clean, modern, but very easy look; there is a certain formality, but it is the formality of line and design rather than of attitude.

"I think that the way we entertain is the way we decorate. We are both collectors and essentially we are always learning about and collecting pieces from different periods; when we do a table therefore we just like to gather together some of the things we have collected—and use them as part of the table. Even though I am no expert in the field, I know what I like, and I want the table to look like an outgrowth of my personal life—not something that has been kept hidden in cupboards and only brought out on occasions—the plan is that we have no plan."

Reed has an antipathy for finished tables that look as if everything on display was bought especially for the occasion: "There is nothing worse than the table looking as if everything on it has come out of a closed cupboard and after the dinner is over, is returned to the cupboard to be hidden from view again. What I find interesting, what gives a table personality, is that everything on it is yours and is on display, and used elsewhere in the house—like the candelabra which usually sits by the fireplace. If it's not something that is part of your life, you shouldn't use it. I want something that is really personal—the plates that I like to use, for instance (and which are on this table) I designed for Bernadout. We have a beautiful and sturdy dining table, originally designed by Charlotte Perriand, so I prefer to use tablemats—in a sharp color like acid yellow or vermilion to add a shot of contrasting color. Lighting should be low, and candlelight is always better. As far as flowers go, rather than having elaborate centerpieces, I go around the house and take them from different vases and put them on the table. Generally speaking, I feel that the idea is to use your life, not let your life use you."

LEFT The restoration of John Saladino's house in Montecito, California, has been a labor of love, with equal emphasis on both words. After stripping out layers of tacky decoration the house has re-emerged as a beautiful butterfly.

RIGHT ABOVE Like all true romantics, John Saladino lays the table with studied care: the cloth is a heavy antique quilted bedcover which has been laid over a darker floor-length cloth.

RIGHT BELOW Silver charger plates set an opulent rich tone, and on top of them white ceramic plates are layered, on which stand glasses of ethereal pudding.

romantic

Romantic style is a question of texture and tone; a romantic table is never hard or edgy, ugly or mean, and will always have an aura of sensuality, sometimes understated, sometimes more overt.

DELICACY AND DISCERNMENT John Saladino is one of America's most famous and successful designers. Corporate spaces, houses, apartments —he does them all, as well as designing his own furniture . . . and, not surprisingly, he also sets a wonderfully rich and welcoming table.

John Saladino is, of course, the master of the romantic style. It colors all his work, although it is tempered with a more severe classicism. "A romantic by nature, a classicist by choice," he says. He is also a magician who can make a simple table transmute into something else, but rather than using spells, he employs imagination and taste in equal parts. As he says, "Sometimes I'm

LEFT A table dressed by John Saladino is guaranteed to amuse, to charm and to give pleasure. These *amuses-bouche* baskets of grapes set on silver salvers are accessorized with delicately wrought silver grape scissors.
OPPOSITE An airy dish of dessert is crowned with a hat of spun sugar. The flowers literally work on two levels—some set high in tall, fragile spires vying with the stately candles so that diners can see below, others set in low, massed softly textured bowls so that diners can see above them.

"Every table is a landscape: and it should be laid out with almost architectural principles."

romantic but I'm always sensual," and at home in Santa Barbara his dining table exemplifies these qualities.

In his dining room, the round table is dressed with a heavy, richly textured almost three-dimensional cloth which is in fact an antique bedspread—"I love the fact that it's old and quilted." On top he has layered plates on silver charger bases—"which gives layers of color to the table."

For John Saladino, "Every table is a landscape: and it should be laid out with almost architectural principles, with the right proportions and scale; each place setting should be surrounded by an invisible hedge so that it is kept, peacefully, on its own. If things do get too crowded, and there is too much on the table, I alter the way the table is set. I might put the napkin over the back of the chair—or if there are too many glasses needed I might re-arrange them in a different way."

The lighting is critical. "The poorest person in the world can afford a few candles—just one votive candle in front of a place makes it special, and emphasizes the separateness of each setting. Sometimes I have very tall candles—18 to 24in (45 to 60cm)—soaring above the diners and then perhaps a chandelier hung way down so that there is a pool of light over the table, like a Renaissance painting where each diner is bathed in a small pool of light." And if that sounds too complicated, he adds some concise advice: "But when in doubt take out all the lights and just have candles."

Flowers should either be chest high, or "way above your head in a giraffe-like vase; at a height where they are on a par with the candles; this way you would have a canopy of flowers and light above you, and you would then do a further more intimate arrangement of small flowers at table level. It's all about scale." And definitely all about romance.

A ROBUST PRETTINESS

Carolyn Quartermaine is a textile and interior designer who has romance written across her heart. Luscious fabrics—silks and satins—and colors like lilac and pink, with everything, but everything, touched with gold, are her signature.

At Carolyn Quartermaine's house in the hills—a village above Cannes—a romantic dining table beneath the olive tree (which she put in when she bought the house two years ago, but which looks as though it has been there for 200 years) is, for her, easy to achieve. Every table setting is a work in progress: "For me setting a table is like trying on a favorite dress or looking at a favorite painting. You follow the mood of the moment; how I live and how I work are very much the same thing to me, so every table reflects what I'm interested in at that moment."

"You could say that my life is a laboratory!" This is particularly the case with her as she usually uses pieces of her own fabrics as tablecloths, on top of which she then adds a mixture—ranging from flea-market finds to inherited treasures. "Any table that I do always includes old pieces— I think that they give interest and depth to an arrangement.' Living in the south, she uses even more color than ever:

OPPOSITE In Carolyn Quartermaine's small walled garden in France, underneath a newly transplanted, but actually extremely venerable olive tree, a table is set for a romantic supper.
RIGHT It is, naturally, all about color: a cream damask cloth, hand painted by Carolyn, is the background for a collection of gilded lusterware bowls and Baccarat glasses.

ABOVE In a deep gilded lusterware bowl is a loosely sprawling bunch of de Vence roses—originally grown for the perfume makers in nearby Grasse and now hard to find in any other parts of the country.

"Any table that I do always includes old pieces—I think that they give interest and depth to an arrangement."

"I love jewel colors down here—topaz, amethyst, and I love to add a touch of fluorescence as well. I no longer have plain glass either—colored glass here is so beautiful with the light coming through it." Quartermaine's romantic table would also always have flowers of some description on it: "It might be a plant though, or it might be a branch with its leaves, an apple or olive branch laid along the center of the table; I have also had a lemon branch with its fruit, and once a branch of mimosa blossom along a white cloth. Blossom is always beautiful, and an olive branch is particularly good as it stays fresh for so long. The whole thing is about balance and scale."

Any romantic table needs romantic lighting, preferably a chandelier, and so Carolyn has one above her table, attached to the branches of the olive tree. "It's important to look at the space above the table—in this case the tree! Don't just focus on the table top—think around it. Note what you have on the walls and in the room. Outdoors, just as much as indoors, lighting is important—use candles on the table in hurricane holders and old oil lamps are good, giving a warm glow across the table and beyond. And don't forget background lighting—tea lights in jars or glasses on the ground or grouped along the top of a wall make everything seem even more romantic."

ABOVE LEFT Inside Carolyn Quartermaine's cool, white-walled house is a fantasy of gold and glass; she prefers to collect only colored glass, and buys individual pieces when she sees them—she owns no complete sets.
BELOW LEFT Texture and depth is added as a backdrop in the rich golden tones of the Quartermaine fabric used on the sofa, as well as the cushions.
OPPOSITE On a beaten metal tray are an old Moroccan bottle and tea glasses—hand-painted rather than printed as so many new ones are. The gold-edged plates, which echo the decoration of the glasses, were found in various flea markets.

classical

A classical table is one that has some reference to cultures of
the past. There may be antique pieces employed, or new objects
inspired by old. The colors are soft and muted, textures rich.

LEFT Diane Fisher-Martinson
uses a folding screen—
decorated suitably subtly in
classical grisaille tones—to
make a romantic eating area
inside a larger space. The
table has an under cloth of
gray flannel covered with an
overlay of a sheer silver
metallic material.
RIGHT The table has been
set with Wedgwood plates
depicting some of Giovanni
Piranesi's famous 18th-
century etchings of Roman
ruins. The glasses are
antique, and have been
amassed over many years;
the decoration is a collection
of ornate silvered seashells.

COOL AND COLLECTED Diane Fisher-Martinson is a stylist and tableware
designer who has long been a collector of everything to do with tables.

"Dinnerware, flatware, stemware, table linens are all obsessions; my cupboards
overflow, and I *love* doing table settings," says Diane Fisher-Martinson of her
generous and luscious tables—a fact which actually is abundantly clear, as the
tables she designs are those of a person who not only knows what she is doing
but also really relishes the pleasure to be taken in setting a table with style and
taste. She is highly skilled at evoking the traditional with a twist; her tables are
layered with linen, and china, objects and glasses—rich, lush and inviting. She
is inspired partly by the past—she loves the baroque, old Venice—and partly by
her enthusiasm for collecting. Texture is very important: on one table she uses
an unusual, heavy cloth of gray flannel—not an automatic choice for many
people—overlaid with a piece of Larsen sheer silver fabric. "I think this would
work wonderfully for a New Year's dinner—silver, shine, candles and sparkle."

"My cupboards overflow, and I *love* doing table settings."

She likes to work from the table upwards, "I start with the tablecloth or mats, and build from there." And her innate skill lies in the way that she puts the different, often disparate, ingredients together—a subtle floor-length cloth as a background, gold-edged plates teamed with antique ivory-handled cutlery and delicate gold-edged glasses from Murano; indeed the whole table reflects the baroque atmosphere of 17th-century Renaissance Europe, with candlesticks found in Rome and even the coasters, fragile, hand-painted eglomise.

Away from the fantasy of the finished table she is practical too—on the subject of flowers, for example: "I do love flowers, but I don't like them to be either too fragrant or too large—I really want to see the person across from me." And she doesn't like artificial lighting: "Lighting is always

candles—the more the better" and preferably these are set into some of her large collection of candlesticks, which she mixes together on the table, often grouping them in the centre in between flowers cut low in glasses and individual miniature vases. Instead of—or sometimes as well as—flowers she loves to decorate the table what might be baldly called table decorations, but in Diane's case might be anything that she feels like using from her collection of treasures. "They are usually antique and can be anything from a pair of old finials to a pretty box, a bust—almost anything that is old and with a patina."

For her every table is important and every setting special: "It has to be, for my friends, and actually even for my husband and me when we dine alone."

OPPOSITE In the living room there is another exotic table—suitable perhaps for Christmas or a feast; it displays hints of Venice at its baroque best. The heavy gold tablecloth and napkins are designs from Diane's former company, while the gold-edged glasses and plates are from Venice.

LEFT Everything on this table speaks of luxury, including the hand-painted *verres églomises* coasters for the water glasses and low silver candlesticks.
ABOVE The ivory-handled knives and forks echo the richness of the plates.

global

Global style is everywhere around us, and nowhere is it more evident nor more successful than when employed at the table. The treasures and colors of other cultures can all be used and enjoyed.

MELTING POT Nathan Turner is a true California boy. An antique dealer, he loves to use both what he owns and what he finds, on tables both in the house and in the garden.

Nathan Turner is a hospitable fellow; when asked how many he likes to have at the table, "the more the merrier" is his cheery reply. Not surprisingly for such a natural host, he likes his tables to be fun and he likes them to have a theme; it might be based on a color which inspires him: "Colors work well in California—it's the Western light that does it."

Other times the inspiration might be another country or culture. "I particularly love ethnic themes because they give me a chance to combine the food with the decoration, and of course allow me to use lots of color which I love.' He does elegant Indian suppers, colorful Mexican parties and—a favorite of his—a Moroccan dinner. "For that I would make a lamb tagine and couscous, and decorate the table accordingly."

For these north African themed dinners a low table is laid with a striking green cloth—except that it probably didn't start life as a tablecloth at all. "If I have a great piece of fabric that will work on the table, I just cut it to fit." In fact he very rarely buys any readymade cloths, preferring to use any piece that catches his eye. "It might be an old curtain

ABOVE Nathan Turner loves to give garden feasts; food from other cultures works perfectly on such occasions. Today it is al fresco Mexico. OPPOSITE He has used color in a very Mexican way, with bright pieces of fabric covering the tables, colored paper flags and sprays of baby oranges crammed into tall stone urns.

RIGHT Lateral thinking is the key to Nathan Turner's outdoor displays. As a contrast to the bright and gay, he uses a painting—old, quiet and subtle—as a background for a table of drinks, the color coming this time from the glassware and the drinks themselves.

"I particularly love ethnic themes because they give me a chance to combine the food with the decoration."

that comes into my antique shop or that I see in another, it might be some old linen that I've found." His napkins are also usually old, with different designs mixed together. Like many people interested in table decoration, he loves glass and china—particularly 19th-century pieces—and he mixes pattern and color with abandon, to great effect.

The background matters of course: "Lighting is super-important; I like to eat by candlelight, and if I do use electric lighting it is always in the background and very dim." Outside he combines as many different lights as possible: candles, hurricane lamps and lanterns—it is all very pretty. The decoration of the table is another aspect that he loves. This means flowers, of course. "I like them to be very natural, and I also love using fruit on the table"—as he has on his Moroccan table, mixing sharp yellow pears with deep red dahlias. Sometimes he goes further into the garden: "I like to use leaves and foliage, and sometimes branches. I have an orange tree in the garden and sometimes bring a branch of that in—with the fruit on of course." Sometimes, in lieu of flowers, he displays shells, coral, stones—anything and everything. He exercises his imagination and places whatever seems right for the moment. As he puts it himself, "Nothing is off-limits for the table."

LEFT Eating inside Nathan Turner's apartment is just as colorful as eating outside. This is a Moroccan feast with low bench seating round an equally low table, which is covered with old green and white fabric with a second piece used as a central runner down the length of the table. Flowers and fruits are mixed together in the colors of the cloths. RIGHT He adds a couple of old Moroccan tea glasses, plates edged with silver and simple elegant silver cutlery at each place setting.

LEFT Stephanie Stokes is a seasoned Asia traveller, whose travels in Cambodia inspired this table. On a rich burnt-orange cloth she has arranged metal Naga candle holders, rattan plate holders, wooden and silver chopsticks and pewter beer mugs. OPPOSITE There are Cambodian vases on the sideboard filled with lotus blossom and even the red-checked napkins are made from Cambodian scarves.

"Flowers give a table life, and every table needs flowers."

A TRAVELLER'S BOUNTY
Stephanie Stokes is one of New York's top interior decorators. She has always collected china and glass from all over the world and has a fine collection of the rare and unusual in her Manhattan apartment, which she uses all the time to create original and arresting table settings.

Stephanie Stokes loves to arrange a table; it gives her a chance to use some of her large collection of china and glass. When she dresses the table for dinner, she pays as much attention to the background as she does to the table. In her dining room is a fine antique mirror above a sideboard and she uses this as a backdrop, always arranging some decorative objects in a way that reflects and complements the setting of the table—in this instance tall brown Cambodian vases and lotus blossoms. She always includes flowers: "Flowers give a table life, and every table needs flowers."

She travels widely and the table shown here reflects one of her recent trips—to Cambodia—furnished with the strange and the beautiful, all laid on a Cambodian cloth. The metal candle holders were copied from a 14th-century example spotted in Phnom Penh Museum. Even the red checked napkins are Cambodian, made from the work scarves commonly worn by Cambodian men.

Everywhere is seen as a collecting opportunity: a recent trip to Syria yielded tablecloths and a wonderful centerpiece for which she paid $15. "Unfortunately it cost $75 to send back to New York, but it's still a wonderful centerpiece!"

Linen is very important, particularly since she prides herself on never repeating a setting. "I own something like sixty tablecloths, which come in very useful, particularly because when I am having a large dinner—for thirty people or so—I set up four separate tables. I have turned against pure white tablecloths, as I find the color is too bright a background for many of the table schemes, and I now prefer ivory, or a soft French blue. I also like a strong color for an undercloth—I am particularly fond of a brown velvet cloth and also a red one, both of which work well at Christmas."

She is, in every sense a mistress of global style, with antique French and English sets, as well as rare Asian and Eastern earthenware and stoneware dishes and vessels.

" Your table reflects who you are as well as your culture."

OPPOSITE In striking contrast
to the formal dinners he
sometimes gives is Rumi Verjee's
Japanese-inspired evening. This
is about shape and texture. The
dishes are all earthenware,
designed and handmade in
Japan, as are the beakers and
the almost organic teapot. The
stainless steel chopsticks and
their stand are in, literally, sharp
contrast, as are the ornate
gilded pudding spoon and fork.
RIGHT Chunky black candles
and over-sized wine glasses
add yet more contrast
of scale and design.

SHOWCASE OF THE WORLD Rumi Verjee knows all there is to know about global style; his store is crowded with china, glass and cutlery designed and made everywhere from Italy to Japan, taking in other nations along the way.

Born in India, brought up in Africa, currently living in England, Rumi Verjee of the London emporium Thomas Goode is global style personified and it is not surprising that "eclectic" is his watchword: "Our lives are eclectic, and my tables are always eclectic too; your table reflects who you are as well as your culture, so in my case, my table will reflect a range of cultures and also of styles."

If Rumi Verjee cannot entirely be described as a minimalist, then he is certainly, in design terms, a fan of the disciplined and the restrained, as is made evident in every room of his contemporary London house. Although he does indeed love to use an ever-changing selection of rich and luxurious tableware when giving formal dinners, he is also very much at home with a style of table that is derived from the East, in particular Japan, a country where sophisticated simplicity is venerated, and he likes to combine dishes and objects that are designed strictly for purpose, relying on their textures and shapes to deliver the impact. He knows that, in global terms, beauty is found not only in the rare and the opulent, but also in the simplicity and subtlety of everyday design.

the collector

Collectors like to use as many elements as possible of their disparate collections; their tables are a fascinating mixture of styles and periods, and all the more charming for that.

LEFT Meredith Etherington-Smith collects—and collects. In the kitchen, against a background of Staffordshire figures and Meissen pugs, on a floral plastic cloth, the table is laid with English majolica and modern glasses.
OPPOSITE Shells are one of her constants and this table is decorated with wildly differing examples of the genre, from shell jugs and salts to the hand-painted plates and the square glass container of the real thing in the center. Leopard-printed mats and antique brown Biot plates complete the picture.

A PERSONAL PASSION Meredith Etherington-Smith is a writer and broadcaster who is also a lifelong collector of china, glass, and decorative tableware, concentrating on the unusual, the pretty and sometimes the downright eccentric.

In Meredith Etherington-Smith's London house, the small downstairs dining room is furnished with a large round table which fills most of the space and makes every dinner an intimate and amusing experience. The food is very important in this house and every table is set to complement what is on the menu that day. A summer menu, for example, with light cold dishes, might be served on a table dressed in green, white and silver, while a winter menu might be served against a background of richer colors. "I do have several sets of china—one an antique Meissen design, another a 19th-century Spode design; then there is a rich Imari design, as well as a modern simple set; I also have an unusual set of

"For me, setting the table is really a little theatrical production."

earthenware dark brown glazed Biot plates which are much more informal and which I use for lunch in the garden. Although I love to collect sets, I do think that you don't really need more than one pattern, as you can easily change the mood of the table with different cloths and different flowers, as well as different decorative objects, like my collection of shells and related ware, which I've always collected and love to use as a centerpiece."

"It's all a question of getting the background right. On the round table, for instance, for lunch, I would not use a cloth at all, so that even if I used the same setting it would look completely different against the wooden table surface." Meredith has a large collection of damask tablecloths: "I have always collected them, and although I think that the only cloth to have for a really formal dinner is white,

I also particularly like finding colored damask—I even have one in buttercup yellow, which is wonderful with the dark brown plates.' She likes to layer cloths—"I put on a large plain one that covers the table completely, and then I layer on top of that another one, which might be an old tea cloth embroidered in colored cottons, or a white drawn-threadwork cloth—which I often put over a colored cloth, if it is an informal occasion."

"For me, setting the table is really a little theatrical production; each one is different from the last, depending on what food you are serving, and what flowers are in season. It's almost a sort of decoration game—you can't re-arrange the furniture on a daily basis, nor re-hang all the pictures, so setting a table is one of the few opportunities you have in the domestic interior to play."

retro

Hard to define in strict terms, retro style is, in essence, a combination of things that have gone before as well as the new, mixed together in a manner that is both appealing and sometimes eccentric.

LEFT Keith Johnson and Glen Senk's style is relaxed, informal, and interesting. Eclectic is the word, for they use at table only that which they like. Blue and white plates are colour-linked to the wonderful fish tureen which dominates the table. In complete contrast, the glasses are 18th-century Irish crystal, but simple in design, not sophisticated. OPPOSITE Old buttoned leather benches are arranged either side of a sturdy rectangular antique table.

CREATING ATMOSPHERE Glen Senk and Keith Johnson are the creative spirits behind the hugely successful store group Anthropologie; constantly searching for new things for the stores, they decorate their homes with original élan.

In Glen Senk and Keith Johnson's comfortable apartment in New York the dining table stands beneath the window in one corner of the room, with deep red buttoned leather banquettes on either side, rather reminiscent of a Paris brasserie or a 19th-century London restaurant. It is a comfortable look, an individual look, and it very much sums up Glen and Keith's attitude to eating and to entertaining. "For us, comfort is the most important thing—that and a complete lack of pretension," says Keith Johnson. He abhors the overdone, the trying-too-hard look. "I think that where the table is concerned, you should avoid the rigid or the too formal. You should mix things together and not try too hard. It's the unexpected that lifts a table setting— the unexpected mixed with a bit of humor." In this instance, the bit of humor is a self-confident blue and white ceramic fish tureen which stands proudly in the center.

Keith Johnson likes to mix patterns—"I know that everyone mixes plates and patterns these days, but I still haven't gotten over it. I do it for the stores as well as at home; it makes people take notice of the table, and it is also a conversation piece, which I think is good."

OPPOSITE There is something intensely original and also very confident about the tables that Keith Johnson and Glen Senk create. They really do use what they like and mix and match old and new styles and periods with abandon. And because of their confidence it works. A lively lunch setting is laid out on an antique table and surrounded by wooden Windsor chairs as well as an eccentric metal chair. RIGHT Part-stencilled plates designed for Anthropologie are teamed with coloured pressed glass and the essential oversized Franch linen napkins that they buy whenever they see them. BELOW Delicious and quirky: a fragrantly steaming pie sits upon its own stand with a rambling design.

"It's the unexpected that lifts a table setting—the unexpected mixed with a bit of humor."

The table includes some beautiful antique cut-glass goblets—an unlikely look perhaps for a lover of low-key looks, but Keith enthuses about this particular element, "They are 18th-century Irish, and I love them because again the design itself is unpretentious compared with very formal antique cut glass; for me they have an almost folksy appeal." Napkins are always large at the Senk–Johnson table: "I love to use very oversized ones—my idea of a napkin could be a small tablecloth for someone else; I also love to use old French dish towels, which I buy in Europe," says Keith.

As for decoration, flowers must also be unpretentious—"from the garden, if I can—if I can't, I don't use them at all." Like almost everyone who is concerned with the pleasures of the table, he loves candlelight—"Of course I do; big pillar candles though, not those itsy-bitsy tapers or tea-lights, and I mix the candlelight with room lighting on a low, low dimmer."

"I think it's a matter of being friendly and not afraid of using something very familiar; guests feel comfortable surrounded by the familiar. Then you can mix in something which is either in bad taste or very modern and innovative. The old quote—every successful room has one thing in it in bad taste—is true. It applies to the table as well—and that's what makes an interesting table."

LEFT Provençal style in the Luberon: at her farmhouse Ebba Lopez uses a lean-to beside the main house as an outdoor dining room. Textiles are her delight and she likes to layer them where she can. Here a floor-length linen cloth is covered with a smaller cream cloth, on which roughly textured woven mats are placed. Beside these are antique linen napkins. The quilted seat cushions are by Linum. OPPOSITE The green mottled glasses are from Provençal glassmaker Biot.

country

Country style is not just confined to a rural setting. It is defined by an authenticity, a lack of excessive decoration and a concentration of color and simple design.

A SCANDINAVIAN AESTHETIC Ebba Lopez is the guiding creative spirit behind Linum, the Swedish company that produces sophisticated but simple textiles, accessories, and cushions in a clear strong palette, all perfect for summer life.

Ebba Lopez lives with her husband Kiko and their children in an idyllic old farmhouse in the Luberon valley in France. Once used for breeding silk worms, the house is built in old stone with vines growing up the walls and a hammock in the garden. From here she runs her company, Linum, and entertains in suitably bucolic Provençal style. Meals outside are taken on a terrace against the wall of the house or in an airy three-sided barn abutting the house.

"I always want to make a pretty table—even if it's only the family. We always have candles—that's the Swedish way—and we have a lot of parties. Because of the business, when it comes to tablecloths and napkins, I am overloaded— so much choice." The settings that she does reflect this: "The settings are always spur-of-the-moment things; I like contrasts—to do dark tables in the summer and pale ones in the winter; I pick flowers from the fields, and roses from the

PREVIOUS PAGES Here is
the full glory of Ebba Lopez's
formal outside supper table,
in the old lean-to barn that
serves as an outdoor dining
room. The table is decorated
in cool colors and, as at
every meal, she uses candles
in abundance; flowers are
always from the garden,
arranged in simple but
striking arrangements.

garden which I mix together. I also use other objects that I have found; on our trips both my husband and I collect shells, stones, pieces of driftwood—anything that pleases us."

The table and its pleasures are enjoyed by both Ebba and Kiko, who works in glass—his are the elegant frosted square glass plates used at dinner, and shown on these pages. "He is very demanding—he does much of the cooking and he's very good so he wants the table to look good too. As our dinners are Mediterranean they always look fresh, and the table reflects that. I use a long undercloth—I have one in black and the other in white—and then, for contrast, I put a smaller, bright tablecloth on top. You don't need to change the tablecloth always

though; even a change of coloured napkins—from white to pink, say, changes the whole look. The actual table that I have is not very beautiful, which is why I always use a cloth, but if the surface were nicer, I would use runners as well—I think they make a very modern look."

"We like to use china that contrasts in color with the food. The food itself is easy down here—there are such wonderful fruits and vegetables that you don't need to do much." Ebba collects both new and old china and mixes and matches it with abandon. She is also a great one for adding things to the table. "I love to put a pretty bowl or a vase down with the other crockery—I have pretty things and I want to use them and the table is the perfect place."

"I always want to make a pretty table—even if it's only the family."

LEFT Same location, very
different table, which
demonstrates how color can
completely change a
table–or, indeed a room. For
lunch, Ebba has used a bold
pink-and-white checked cloth
from Linum, emphasized the
color with the food and
the flowers, and then toned
it down with linen cushions,
contrasting the vibrant pinks
with cool greens: smaller
check napkins, green clover-
leaf side plates and vases.
OPPOSITE The beautiful
frosted square glass plates
are by Kiko Lopez.

A SUBTLE AND SOOTHING PALETTE Nicolette Schouten is a formidably successful interior designer, whose company, Collection Privée, is based in both Cannes and Valbonne. Her decorating style is colored by the Mediterranean.

There is a formality in French entertaining that is central to their way of life. But entertaining in southern France is not like that of the north; there, the light is softer, the air balmier, and the weather warmer. In her house overlooking the bay of Cannes, Nicolette Schouten has a dining area that is part of the same room as the kitchen and living area, but partly hidden around the corner so that the food preparation cannot be seen. It opens onto a terrace and the swimming pool. The long table itself is made from old wood in a traditional French country style and comes from her shop in Cannes. When she entertains guests for lunch or dinner in this part of the house, she lays the table with a certain formality, but one with an informal air—a style that uses natural materials and comfortable, easy-to-handle tableware but a table nevertheless that is set out in a traditional and formal manner.

In the strong light of the Mediterranean it is soft, old colors that work well: grays, greens, creams, all mixed together in a relaxing palette that is conducive to eating. The plates, for example, are a soft French gray—a surprisingly good background color for the food. And the food is important

LEFT Nicolette Schouten sets out lunch in the dining hall of her house in Cannes overlooking the sea; her natural preference is for a cool, pale and neutral palette which acts as a calm contrast to the strong light and vibrant colors of the surrounding Mediterranean landscape.
OPPOSITE Neutral does not however mean boring, as is shown by this set of Porcelaine Blanche pale gray and taupe dishes on rough textured gray mats from Collection Privée, highlighted with gray tinted glasses.

OPPOSITE The sophisticated rustic style is set by the table—one of Collection Privée's clever ideas. The table itself is new, but copied from an old design and made up in pieces of aged oak; it can be made up to 10ft (3m) long. LEFT Nicolette adds color to the table with the flowers and the food, both of which she feels look better against a background of neutral tones.

BELOW The heavy woven chairs are from Collection Privée, as are the circular metal chandeliers furnished with sturdy candles which hang low over the table, and are balanced by antique wall lights. At the end of the space is a painting by Linda Biales which pulls the room together.

"I love it when there are lots of things on the table—flowers, candles; sometimes there is almost no room for the food."

to Nicolette: "For me it is very important that the first course and the main course are served correctly and at the right moment; after they have arrived, I relax a little and let go—then I concentrate on the atmosphere rather than the food. When we eat we can go on for hours—that, for me, is a successful dinner." The atmosphere is much enhanced by the way she lays the table. "For a start, I love lots and lots of candles—even in the daytime; music is important, as are flowers. I like everything to be cozy—warm really, definitely not cold."

Hers is not a minimal look: "I love it when there are lots of things on the table—flowers, candles; sometimes there is almost no room for the food, and then my husband goes round removing things!" Her decorator background means that she loves to do color-themed tables, using her chosen palette as far and definitively as possible, from the napkins to the flowers.

Like many who are as interested in the meal itself as the table she does not like scent—either in candles, or flowers, as they detract from the delicious scents of the food. She does however like incense sticks, which she burns in small groups around the room and on the terrace. Her style is a blend of the old and the new—a style that comes from respect for the wellbeing and enjoyment of her guests.

meal times

OUR INFORMAL MEALS—breakfast, lunch, supper at home—are designed to be the very opposite of the formal feast, and are usually presented accordingly. At home, the table is set, on a daily basis, in a way that is dependent on the meal that has been planned and the practicalities involved therein. Over twenty-four hours there are many very different types of meals that might be taken—from the simplest of breakfasts (which might well be a far more elaborate production on the weekend) to a light lunch with friends, afternoon tea as a treat, perhaps, and later an informal supper at home, or on occasions, a formal dinner party or a larger feast.

There are increasing levels of complexity between these different occasions, and they influence, sometimes subconsciously, the thought behind your selection of everything from the china and glass to linen and any table decoration you might choose.

It is very easy to slide into a practical, and speedy, rut where setting the table every day is concerned. Anyone can set a table with its most basic necessities—same old plates, glasses and linen—but what is more fun, for the setter as well as those sharing the meal, is to lay the table using a bit of alternative thinking. Eschewing the obvious and looking at schemes related by color, perhaps, or pattern; exploring the back of the crockery cupboard for some plates or bowls not often used; looking at alternatives to the usual tablecloth or glasses—in other words, using a bit of imagination and a little flair— can elevate the every day into something that is both stylistically and personally interesting rather than mundane and uninspiring.

OPPOSITE Ebba Lopez sets a table inside her Provençal farmhouse that is a symphony in gray. On a background of a gray and black striped cloth by Linum, she adds mottled gray plates, gray napkins, smoked gray glasses and even gray candles, set off with tumblers of gray-green rosemary from the garden. PREVIOUS PAGES Any meal can be given a sense of occasion when thought and care go into both the decoration and the food. This wonderfully inviting table is by Gilles and Marianne Pellerin.

breakfast

For many people breakfast is the most important meal of the day and also the one to which they look forward with most relish. It is also one of the nicest meals to make a little effort with, as it holds promise of good things to come.

In times past breakfast was not a leisurely meal; it was, as its name implied, the breaking of the fast of the night before. Historically the last meal meal of the day would been eaten much earlier in the evening than it is today, so people would have gone for a longer period without eating and would wake up in much greater need of refreshment. Breakfast provided the initial fuel for the working day ahead and was substantial—although many people, such as farm workers, put in a couple of hours of work before breakfast was eaten, and so would have built up quite an appetite. By the 19th century, generally speaking, the later you ate breakfast, the

more leisured your lifestyle, and today we tend to have two sorts of breakfasts: the get-up-and-go start to the day ones and the weekend and holiday breakfasts where the meal becomes an event—a low-key, leisurely, delightful and relaxing event that sets the tone for the day ahead.

Even—actually, particularly—if you are having breakfast on your own, it really is worthwhile making it look nice—as François Gilles, who sets his breakfast table with care in a sunny corner says, "The breakfast table should be peaceful and calm. I am a slow mover in the morning, and I need a gentle start. You need a clear mind to arrange a

OPPOSITE, FAR LEFT Abigail Ahern, owner of the contemporary home gallery and shop in London Atelier Abigail Ahern, sets a calm, neutral breakfast table using black stoneware dishes, a Rupert Spiro milk jug and a collection of old gray glass French beer bottles.
OPPOSITE, ABOVE RIGHT Breakfast set outside is always the best start to a day, if the weather is right.

OPPOSITE, BELOW LEFT Designed for company When Objects Work by John Pawson, these white breakfast bowls are the very essence of simplicity.
BELOW In Stefan and Kristof Boxy's house outside Ghent, the welcoming fruit-laden breakfast table is completed by wild strawberries laid on a heavy lead crystal indented dish designed by Clarissa Berning.

day, and I like to sit down and think at breakfast in a pleasant atmosphere surrounded by crockery and things that I like, including the rug, which reminds me of my house in Morocco."

Abigail Ahern, owner of cutting edge shop Atelier Abigail Ahern in London, uses contemporary designs and contrasting colors and shapes, while Carolyn Quartermaine often takes her breakfast in the sun and uses correspondingly sunny colors and shapes on her breakfast table on a bright roof terrace in France.

If the breakfast is to be a sociable one, with friends invited to join you, and has even segued into brunch, slightly later in the morning, it is important that the table should look welcoming at first glance. Possibly one of the easiest ways to achieve that is to have already set out on the table some tangible indication of the pleasures to come in the form of food—something edible always looks more inviting than a bare table or one laid only with crockery and cutlery. It may be as simple as a loaf of fresh bread, a basket of croissants or buns, a bowl of fruit or even some jams in their own jars, or decanted into bowls or open jars—each with its own spoon and on a plate or saucer. Individual butter pots are good for silent eaters, along with pretty glasses for juice.

The choice of china—and glass—is more important than you might think. Because breakfast is a slightly contemplative meal, people often take time to consider

the cups—which should be large enough for a decent cup of tea or coffee—and the plates or bowls. Cheerful colors are good, particularly on gray mornings, and a bright tablecloth is a good start. (Even those purists for whom a white cloth is otherwise *de rigeur* will allow a touch of color at the breakfast table). The same goes for napkins, which could contrast with the cloth, and should be large enough to cope with coffee and crumbs.

Simple flowers are always preferable at breakfast—particularly if they are freshly picked from the garden with a touch of dew still on them; the breakfast table is not a place for statement-making blooms.

A CHEERFUL START A bright tablecloth is the background for designer Voon Wong's breakfast table. He trained as an architect, which helps to explain his fluid ceramic style.

In partnership with Benson Saw, he has designed an innovative and adaptable range of beautifully light-reflective bone china vessels in amorphous, delicate shapes which have been made for them by one of China's largest manufacturers of bone china. There are three different combinations of what they call condiment dishes: linked, rounded shapes; a large circular hors d'ouevre dish with indentations of different sizes; as well as an almost sculptural dish with many points. Using them he sets breakfast at his London studio as a very casual affair, using bowls of differing sizes and some of his linked condiment dishes. The cleverness of the design means all is placed conveniently close to hand.

ABOVE The contemporary bone china designs by the company Voon Benson combine the delicacy of traditional bone china pieces with sculptural, almost architectural shapes.
BELOW Simple bowls and plates are combined with dishes that look like unfolded handkerchiefs, set out on a cloth of cheerful, morning-welcoming stripes.

OPPOSITE Small, linked condiment dishes, reminiscent of raindrops or clouds, hold all the culinary necessities of the perfect indulgent breakfast.

OPPOSITE On a smoothly polished wooden table Keith Johnson and Glen Senk use plates from their company Anthropologie that are both stenciled and painted, and combine them with pressed glass tumblers and jug. RIGHT Lunch at the home of Gilles and Marianne Pellerin in the south of France is a cool, laid-back affair. A series of small cold dishes are arranged the length of a table from Collection Privée that is made from old wood.

lunch

It is always pleasant to take a brief interlude in the middle of the day to refresh oneself and catch up with friends before embarking on the rest of the day's activities, or enjoy a pitstop at which all the family gather together.

Lunch is a relative newcomer to the history of eating. Dinner and supper were what was originally eaten—with dinner falling in the middle of the day. Supper was a light bite before going to bed—which most people, other than the very rich, did earlier than they do now, candles being expensive luxuries, beyond the reach of many working families. By the late 18th and early 19th centuries, dinner had crept backwards, supper was only served at long evening occasions, and to fill the often rather long gap between breakfast and dinner, luncheon crept in.

The concept of 'ladies who lunch' is not new—in the 1800's women entertained each other at light luncheons, occasions at which men were rarely present. That may have changed but we still look on lunch—except for specific occasions like the Sunday lunch or weekend lunch parties—as a lighter meal. Generally fewer courses are served; indeed recipe books still give ideas for dishes that could be either "first courses or a light lunch dish." So the luncheon table is usually more lightly dressed than the corresponding dinner table, with less attendant formality, and is often arranged for the diners to be more or less self-serving.

In the 19th century there was a distinct difference between the formal dinner tablecloth—always white and always damask—and the type of cloth considered suitable

for the lunch table; the table, often a prized family possession, would be covered with a cloth that was worked with lace panels, or pierced, cutwork decoration, or even set with a rectangular runner—all designed to let the polished surface of the table be seen.

Runners are again popular; Abigail Ahern, who hates formality in a table, no matter what the occasion, is a big fan of the runner, and on her own table uses an original design in ridged felt; in France, Ebba Lopez likes to use runners on outdoor tables, as does Marianne Pellerin, who uses several horizontally, rather than vertically, across the table.

Relative informality in the design of dishes and plates is also traditionally part of the lunchtime experience. Serving dishes used to be designed either with rims—intended for use at dinner—or without, for lunch. Earthenware and stoneware plates were considered suitable materials for employing at midday meals, while the finer porcelain was reserved for the formal meal of the day—dinner.

Abigail Ahern feels that this applies just as much today as it did yesterday: "I hate formal tables for lunch, although flowers are absolutely fundamental, as are tea lights around the room as well as on the table. I much prefer a degree of the impromptu, and I love using hand-thrown dishes like these from potter Davda which are very simple shapes, in natural glazes." She likes to mix those with other designs—she has a horror of the matching—"I like every place to be different." She serves "really simple, easy food that is neither complicated nor fussy. The thing about great tableware is that it makes the food look so good."

ABOVE LEFT Ebba Lopez, in France, arranges a Provençal lunch outside. On a rough, deep-dyed indigo cloth traditional earthenware pots hold baby *saucisses*, olives and earthy sauces.
RIGHT Abigail Ahern likes a casual relaxed lunch table; a corrugated felt runner is striking and contrasts with the very simple hand-glazed dishes by Davda in a range of subtle, natural colors.

LIGHT SUMMER LUNCH
Interior designer Marianne Pellerin is married to Gilles Pellerin, an architect, and their house in the hills above Cannes is a glowing testament to their combined professional skills.

They sometimes eat their lunch in the garden, but when the midday Mediterranean summer sun beats down, it is cooler and more congenial to eat in the cool dining room, which leads out onto the terrace.

The long table, made from old wood, is laid with mats and on top of them is set a series of plates in slightly different shapes—some square, and others circular. Although the china varies in color each piece is within the particular color palette that Marianne likes to use: "Always shades of gray, taupe and cream as they are perfect background colors and are also calm and cool. It is important that nothing should trouble the eye, detract from what we are going to eat; for that reason I also keep the lighting subdued, with the table a candle-lit pool of light against a dark background."

Flowers that have been cut low—lilies, hydrangea heads, roses, and all white—are displayed in clear glass vases and arranged down the length of the table. "I always keep flowers low so that people can talk over them, and I decide on the color of the flowers according to the menu." It is very pretty, but—according to Marianne—is not complete: "A table is not a set table until the food is on it; however good it looks, it is not finished without the food." This means that the food must complement the dishes and vice versa, which, of course, it does. "The china is the perfect color for the strong colors of the Mediterranean food that we love to eat, which is very south of France, vegetable based and with many small plates to choose from. As long as that combination is right, everything else will work too."

> "A table is not a set table until the food is on it; however good it looks, it is not finished without the food."

LEFT For Marianne Pellerin the essential element of any table setting is the food itself, and everything—china, glasses and cutlery—are chosen to complement and highlight this.
OPPOSITE Square white ruffle-edged plates of graded sizes from Porcelaine Blanche in Cannes, which throw the brightly colored roasted vegetables into strong contrast, are combined with drinking glasses from Mulberry and rough-textured taupe tablemats.
ABOVE Flowers in the Pellerin household are discreet and often white.

afternoon tea

The concept of afternoon tea as a social occasion became both fashionable and popular in the mid-19th century, so much so that the tea-gown, a day-dress that was much lighter than a morning or walking dress, became an established part of a fashionable lady's wardrobe.

Afternoon tea should not be confused with high tea; the latter is a substantial meal which developed, mainly in the north of England, as the equivalent of dinner at the end of a working man's day and was served around 5 or 6 pm. Afternoon tea is a very different affair—a light meal where one or more teas are served, traditionally an Indian tea and a China tea, the latter being more delicate in flavor than the former. Today, a herbal tea might also be offered, although purists might demur.

The traditional culinary accompaniment to the tea—the latter always made in a teapot—would be thin, buttered, crustless triangular sandwiches of

white or brown bread, with fillings such as sliced cucumber, egg and watercress, and liverpaste.

After the Second World War, the ritual of afternoon tea seemed to decline into a drink taken in a mug with a teabag; now the whole procedure—or even ceremony—seems to be reviving in popularity, which is good news as it is one of the simplest and nicest ways of entertaining. Pretty tea cups, often collected in ones and twos, small tea cloths—once popular and still to be found in garage sales and in market stalls—laid on a table inside or outside the house; what could be nicer?

Tricia Foley wholeheartedly agrees: "I usually serve three different pots of tea—one black, one green, and then an infusion of some description. There are usually cucumber sandwiches, Cheddar with chutney and one of herbs and garden sprigs. The bread is really thin—and sometimes there is shortbread too. Yes, I make it an occasion—I think that if you ask people to tea, you should do it properly."

OPPOSITE, ABOVE LEFT AND BELOW On the deck of her dock house, Tricia Foley sets out a summer tea, with the teapot and cups placed on a side table set against the wall of the house. The combination of sunshine and cucumber sandwiches is irresistible.

OPPOSITE, ABOVE RIGHT For a very traditional teatime, Glen Senk and Keith Johnson use whatever is to hand that is both attractive and useful: a white china teaset, an old glass cake stand and blue-and-white cups fit the bill.

BELOW In the sitting room of Tricia Foley's Long Island house, everything is ready for a very chic cup of tea and something sweet to eat. Tricia collects creamware new and old which she mixes together, along with black basalt ware. Collections of glass and ceramics are arranged on the mantelpiece and cupboard top.

SWEET TREATS AND POSIES If there is one sort of tea party that is worth making a fuss over it is a tea party for children—whether it is two or ten, the reward ratio is high indeed, particularly if you have taken some time and trouble to arrange a table that will please.

Louise Nason, owner of London chocolate store Melt and therefore the Chocolate Queen, always makes an effort when she sets out a child-sized table with everything that a child (probably a girl) would like to see. Naturally, this includes flowers. Nason likes to serve small portions of brightly colored food, savory first with sweet things afterwards—which might be fairy cakes, a little fruit and naturally something in chocolate, such as a doe-eyed chocolate Bambi. Sometimes she adds a small present, like a set of miniature wooden pastry-making utensils, tied in ribbon. "Keep it

simple, and don't go over the top," is her advice, particularly where the tablecloth is concerned, as drinks invariably get knocked over. One clever solution might be to have a heavy white paper cloth with a small set of crayons at every seat.

"Keep it simple, and don't go over the top."

OPPOSITE Tea for Louise Nason's children and friends is set out on a small-sized table with correspondingly small chairs. A floor-length pink checked cotton cloth is a pretty and practical cover.
LEFT Individual portions of sweet treats are attractively presented in miniature white bowls with suitably child-sized spoons.
ABOVE It would almost be a shame to eat such an appealing figure as this chocolate fawn, but it is so delicious no child could resist!

dinner

Is it called dinner or is it called supper? If it's dinner is it eaten in the middle of the day or in the evening? And if in the evening at what time is it served—6 pm? 7? 8 or later?

Historically dinner was the main, heaviest meal of the day, served in the middle of the day, with a light snack—usually referred to as supper—served just before retiring in the evening. Bed time for most was usually far earlier than it is today, due mainly to the fact that very few people had access to, or money for, candle or lamp light by which to use the evening profitably.

As the centuries passed, cheaper lighting and more leisure time meant bedtime became later, particularly for the moneyed upper and professional classes; and dinner therefore became later too. By the mid 18th century it was served at around 3 or 4 pm and by the 19th century it was anchored in the early evening, where for many people, it still remains today—give or take an hour or two.

Supper as an extra meal has all but disappeared, but the word is now often used instead of dinner to indicate an alternative evening meal, one which—if friends are invited—will be very much less formal than a dinner; dinner often now has the connotation of a formal party—see our section later in the book. Dinner or supper is still the meal to which we most often ask our friends, being the part of day when—theoretically—work is over and the time has arrived to relax and

ABOVE The ways in which a dinner table is presented are many and multifarious— if you are serving Asian food it makes sense for the whole of the setting to reflect an Eastern theme. OPPOSITE This dinner setting is uncompromisingly contemporary and equally Scandinavian influenced, with Finnish glass and Swedish plates. The mats are black, heavy and ridged —a contrast to the smooth, pale wooden table.

LEFT Ebba Lopez is incapable of not using color cleverly. She even, almost by instinct, seems to choose to serve food that complements the colors of the table.
OPPOSITE François Gilles is a collector as well as a decorator; this dinner table, inspired both by the 1950s and the colors and textures of Morocco, is dressed with quirky ceramic pieces by Anne Stocke.
BELOW Voon Wong's adaptable new ceramic range works just as well on the dinner table as at breakfast. His clever simple plates and bowls and linked sets of small dishes are reflected against a high-shine black table.

talk and eat good food. There are few nicer invitations than to be asked to come and eat in the evening and the setting of an attractive and welcoming table is a major part of the whole experience.

The central difference between an informal dinner and a formal one is a sense of ease—both in the food and in the settings. Glen Senk and Keith Johnson, for example, both stress this with their emphasis on comfort and lack of pretension, as does designer Ebba Lopez with her dinner in the kitchen, where the table is set with striking linens and china, but in which any possible formality is offset by the coziness of the surrounding kitchen. Writer Meredith Etherington-Smith emphasizes the informal and the amusing—both welcome elements of the informal dinner—when she sets the table with shell *objets* and leopard print tumblers, as does interior designer François Gilles, who is so passionate about color and design that his bright, Moroccan-inspired dining table sings with a spontaneous splash of color and pattern.

Dinner for designer Voon Wong is a relaxed affair, a meal which is Asian in concept—perhaps Vietnamese, where a salad of noodles might be accompanied by various side dishes of meat and vegetables. His clever range of bone china hors-d'oeuvres dishes and linked condiment dishes encourage the idea of easy eating—as he says, "Casual, but proactive!"

MONOCHROME DINING In contrast to the idea of color and yet more color is the architect and designer John Pawson's minimalist take on domestic life; to further his view he has designed for Beatrice Delafontaine's company "When Objects Work," a range of simple, but incredibly clever tableware.

The cutlery—a knife, fork and spoon—he originally designed as part of his mammoth architectural project, a new monastery for the Cistercian Order in Romania, where he observed the monks' use of their personal cutlery, which they brought to table wrapped in a napkin and which, after use, they washed and rewrapped. He wanted to design something equally simple, and good looking.

Pawson has also designed a tableware range which includes, along with large bowls and candle holders, a perfectly shaped mug and a reversible plate—in white, of course. Stefan and Kristof Boxy are two of Belgium's best young chefs who have turned from running their own starred restaurant to running a catering company cooking for events and parties. Pawson's designs are the perfect backdrop for their delicious and beautifully presented food. Serving their appetizing dishes in this manner adds to the drama—and fun—of the dinner.

Beatrice Delafontaine herself was taught about setting the table by the rigorous rules of her grandmother: "She taught me that the first impression of the table is very important, and she showed me how to ensure that the handles of the knives and forks at each place setting touched the edge of the table. To be comfortable, each setting should be about 24–28in (60–70cm) in width, which allows for general conversation with other guests." She feels that form is more important than color, which is evident in this elegant setting.

"At dinner you should be able to have a conversation with most of the people around you."

OPPOSITE AND ABOVE John Pawson's tableware is striking and effective. The plate, called, unsurprisingly, "plate/dish" does exactly what it says, with one side inverted to form a shallow bowl, here filled with a dish of sweetbreads garnished with chocolate, the other side flat enough to hold a fantasy of langoustine. The water glass and goblet are unadorned and easy to hold, the cutlery functional and good looking.
RIGHT The Boxy brothers' dining room, a space in the garden designed by the late Maarten van Severen, is divided from the kitchen with mirrored panels, as well as a continuous wall of glass that extends to the length of the kitchen beyond.

DECORATING A DINNER TABLE Vicente Wolf is polymath man. An accomplished author and photographer, he is also a very successful and prolific designer, based in New York where he designs not only very cool, very clean interiors, but also furniture, textiles, china and flatware.

In Vicente Wolf's summer home in Montauk, everything is geared towards relaxed summer life, and that includes the way that the tables are designed and set. "Everything that I do in this house is about playing—here I have time to think about the tables and to inject a bit of fantasy and romance into the decoration."

He has always been a great traveler and collector—of everything from black-and-white photographs to golden-skinned Buddhas—but he is perhaps unusual in that his collections are not arranged just to be admired as objects in themselves but are also brought into use to decorate and embellish every aspect of the house.

On his dining table, for example, dotted around the place settings, which consist of china and sterling silver flatware that he has himself designed, he loves to use a collection of oddly shaped small blue glass bottles that he has found over the years. "I think collections choose us, rather than us choosing them; with these bottles I first started buying them in local yard sales; next a thrift shop in nearby Bridgehampton yielded a few more, and then I started to buy them from all around the world, everywhere from Paris and Amsterdam to the Middle East. When you start to see a lot of these little bottles together you realize that the blue in the glass reflects the colors of the summer light here as well as that of the ocean."

"I fill the bottles with flowers that I have brought in from the garden, and because each bottle is different, the whole table looks effusive but not fussy; it's a different way of arranging flowers and it works in a way that wouldn't have worked had I used lots of little vases in different colors. That way, it would have been too fussy— this way there is a unity and it doesn't become too decorator-like. One of the few cases, I think, where more is definitely more."

ABOVE Not only is Vicente Wolf a designer of interiors, he also designs furniture, as well as table and flatware, of which the place setting here is a fine example.

LEFT Vicente Wolf always combines the simple and the sophisticated; an "'effusive" table, he calls this one— definitely a case of where more is better.
OPPOSITE The table with its heavy white cloth and draped dining chairs are a fine background for the decoration, casually placed photographs and some of his collection of small, unusual glass bottles.

"Everything that I do in this house is about playing."

outdoor eating

Eating out of doors is an experience in itself. In our minds outdoor daytime dining is always taken in weather that is balmy rather than uncomfortably hot, sunny without being enervating, with the scents and sounds of summer around us.

An evening outdoors, we see as one under a starlit sky, lit by soft, glowing candles and lanterns with the scent of evening flowers all around. Of course the reality—particularly for those of us who live in northern climates—is often far from this ideal, but that doesn't mean that the lure of outdoor dining doesn't call to us all. There are several prerequisites for eating outdoors. The first is that the seating—whether it is cushions and blankets on the grass, or upholstered chairs—should be comfortable; artless simplicity can only go so far. The second is that there should be some means of shading the table, whether natural or imported; a sunny summer's day can sometimes be unpleasantly bright. The third thing is that the food, albeit attractively presented, should, in the main, be as simple as the setting.

All aficionados of eating outdoors like to arrange something special on the table. Stylist Diane Fisher-Martinson has gone so far as to build a pergola in her Long Island garden, where she and her husband, also a gardener, can take a "luncheon for gardeners." They

designed a large limestone and iron table that can be left outside all year round. In the garden there are groves of bamboo and they repeat the bamboo theme in the chargers, mats, flatware and even the thermos when setting the table. Instead of flowers, they use herbs in tin pots and antique terracotta flowerpots. Nicolette Schouten in France also likes to eat beneath a pergola at a large round table, furnished with a permanent revolving Lazy Susan. For more intimate meals, she uses a small table in another part of the garden, which is naturally shaded by a large old olive tree.

Carolyn Quartermaine's tiny garden in the French hills is another outdoor dining area which she uses for both lunch and dinner, mixing and matching according to the time and the weather. Also, in the south of France, where eating outdoors is after all a much more usual occurrence, Marianne Pellerin has installed a table on a terrace near the swimming pool, which overlooks the bay of Cannes—a patchwork of twinkling light at night. Rather than using a wayward tablecloth, she uses runners, laid horizontally, with small but heavy flower holders at either end of the table. A small and very convenient kitchen has been built into the

OPPOSITE On the far side of her garden, overlooking the bay of Cannes, Nicolette Schouten has built a large circular pergola, over which wisteria has been trained. Beneath it is an oversized stone and metal table that seats 12 people comfortably, with, at its center, a large, stone 'Lazy Susan' which spins delicious dishes round within reach of the diners.

ABOVE LEFT Nicolette keeps the location simple under the pergola; the setting and the views need no competition.
ABOVE RIGHT This is not a grand gesture setting—it is all about a relaxed lunch on a summer's day, with antique china and traditional furniture.

LEFT The pergola under which Nicolette Schouten arranges her al fresco feasts is at the end of a long tunnel of cool greenery that weaves beside the swimming pool.

adjacent pool house. Across the Atlantic, on the sometimes windy terrace of her contemporary house on Long Island, tableware designer Peri Wolfman has perfected the art of the beautiful, wind-proof table. A heavy, and therefore relatively unblowable (and washable) Marseilles quilt is used as a tablecloth, and stones from the beach are used as both graphic table decorations and highly effective weights.

Nathan Turner uses his garden in California for themed feasts, one of the main requisites of which is that they should be both colorful and fun, and festooned with lanterns and lights. Agnès Emery, one of Belgium's most successful designers, is a true artist, who produces not only innovative interior design, but also ceramic, wallpapers, fabric and glass. For her, a meal outdoors is almost a painterly study and it starts first and foremost with the food; once she has chosen what the menu will be she then carefully chooses not only the dishes that will complement and flatter, but also which textiles to use on the table and the glasses and decanters that will work best. It is the combination of color and texture that is so important—that and, of course, the pleasure of the meal itself.

ABOVE AND RIGHT Peri Wolfman likes to eat outside at her Long Island home. The cloth is actually a Marseilles quilt—it is heavy enough not to blow away and is easily washable. The table decoration is a group of beach finds, including pebbles that also help to anchor the cloth. Large blue-and-white napkins add a touch of colour.
OPPOSITE In France Marianne Pellerin sets up an Eastern–Western lunch table on a poolside terrace. The glass table is covered with runners arranged horizontally on which rectangular Asian-inspired dishes of different sizes are set.

LEFT The tables that John Saladino sets are always both decorative and extremely comfortable, whether they are laid indoors or out.
RIGHT Here, on a terrace, a wooden high-backed bench is stacked with cushions and the round, stone table is decorated with simple plates, very decorative china-handled knives and fragile iridescent glasses; flowers are simple, garden blooms and foliage, arranged in a glass.

COMMUNING WITH NATURE As well as living in Manhattan, where he loves to eat in the garden "to smell the flowers and hear the birds," John Saladino also has a beautiful early 20th-century house in California, in the hills above Santa Barbara, which he has been restoring.

There is garden a-plenty and he makes generous use of it by setting up several areas blessed with wondrous views, furnished with tables, chairs and seats—perfect places for tea, drinks, lunch or supper.

"The thing about eating outdoors is that you can be much more casual than when you eat inside. You can have comfortable seats, piled with cushions, you can use pottery instead of porcelain and use more amusing, brighter colors. Reserve the best crystal and silver for inside the house—it really is not appropriate to have silver outdoors," says Saladino. This is a good thing because it means you can use other, unusual cutlery, such as the painted china-handled knives on the round table set for lunch here. Simple flowers too—preferably from the garden and displayed in tumblers or small vases. Marble or stone make good table tops for the garden, and need no cover, but if you

> "The thing about eating outdoors is that you can be much more casual than when you eat inside."

OPPOSITE The paper doily, long dismissed as an old-fashioned irrelevance, is brought smartly back into fashion by John Saladino, using them as he does here, as an extra decorative layer between a simple plate and the dessert dish. RIGHT It's all in the detail where John is concerned. For him, large napkins are essential, and this cut-work hemmed design is both pretty and practical.

prefer a cloth, John Saladino suggests that you can use an old bedspread or a pretty length of colorful fabric rather than a conventional white tablecloth.

Outside is the place to have fun with some decorative centerpieces too: "Perhaps a pile of sand in the middle of the table, in which you could hide small pots of chives, so that the chive stalks look like clumps of grass in the desert. And if you are serving seafood, scatter some shells around the table and fill a couple with cheap pearl ropes."

Use decorative objects that pertain to the place—small, old terracotta flowerpots perhaps, filled up with waxed paper and then topped with grapes or cherries spilling over from the top. And think about using vegetables, which are less

commonly used for decoration than fruit. "Things like fennel have such a strong architectural shape and look wonderful in a bowl; or bunches of asparagus, tied in bundles with string or ribbon, and lined up on the table— the bonus being that you can eat them the next day!"

Always inventive and imaginative, Saladino brims with ideas for decorating the table with items taken from the house. "If you are on a budget, take some things that you already own, and use them on the table. Think laterally: for example—what about some toy soldiers lined up as if they were on dress parade; make a small scene and add other pieces of militaria to the group." John Saladino's message is simple—it's summer, it's outdoors—have fun.

BELOW The message in these particular bottles is that this is a table with a seaside theme, albeit no closer to the sea than Alison Price's London garden. As well as ships-in-bottles, there are shell-printed runners, which Alison found by chance, and white napkins (Alison's favorite napkin color), embellished with a single shell.

RIGHT The table itself is scattered with a combination of real and ornamental shells, while other shells have a practical function, used as individual pepper and salt holders. A tall exuberant centerpiece of hydrangeas is balanced with small vases of white blooms at table level.
OPPOSITE The marine theme extends to the food: crayfish salad is served in simple white dishes.

SUMMER LUNCH IN A CITY GARDEN Alison Price, creator of beautiful parties, large and small, lives in the country as well as the town, and outdoor life and its attendant pleasures are very important to her.

Originator of some of the prettiest tables in London, Alison Price has a small garden at her London house which she treats like an outdoor dining room and uses a lot. "When you eat out of doors, although the table should look—and be— far less formal than a table indoors it is important to make it just as pretty and attractive. The basics are of course still very important, and you must make the whole setting comfortable, with chairs that you can relax in and a table that is large enough. The table setting should be eye-catching, but also relatively simple, and the food should be seasonal. The thing outside is not to be over-clever."

This summer lunch is a romantic fantasy furnished with a round table that she dresses with naturalistic care, incorporating everything from driftwood to shells, crowned with a centerpiece of carefully arranged hydrangea blooms. She buys interesting pieces constantly, wherever she sees them, to use at her garden table and hangs candles in jars and pretty lanterns from the garden trees and shrubs. Decorating a table, inside and out, is about using your life as a backdrop.

picnics

Picnics have been enjoyed by hunters and other sportsmen for hundreds of years, but it was not until the early 19th century—as documented by Jane Austen in her description of her heroine Emma's eagerly anticipated picnic on Box Hill—that picnics came to be seen as enjoyable, companionable occasions to be arranged and organized with as much care as any other social event. Perhaps though, with too much care: the picnic that is served with as much finesse as a formal dinner party, guests seated at a conventional table, complete with the very best porcelain and other refinements is perhaps something that has moved away from the spirit of what a picnic should really be. As Vicente Wolf says, "Picnics are about getting away—so don't travel with too much luggage."

In principle the perfect picnic is an informal, social occasion that allows the guests to enjoy a charming aspect of the surrounding landscape—which may be marine, rural, set in a city park, or even take place within your own garden. The point is that it is a time to relax, sitting on rugs or cushions while enjoying a delicious meal of portable food and drink that is light, summery, and delicious.

Rumi Verjee likes to compose picnics in his London courtyard garden where, surrounded by trees and grass, it is quite easy to imagine oneself being far away. Vicente Wolf is a big fan of picnics and at his house in Montauk he likes to create pastoral fantasies such as the imaginative and delicate picnic he has set up beneath an overflowing flowering tree. A mosquito net that is not only ethereally pretty but also practical, has been attached to the branches of the tree. "When the wind blows, the netting moves. I love that because it transports you and it's a way of transporting your guests"—what a neat definition of picnic life.

ABOVE AND BELOW RIGHT Rumi Verjee of Thomas Goode sets out a traditional and very glamorous picnic tea in the courtyard garden of his London house, complete with hand-painted Hering tea cups, Meissen tea and coffee pots, and golden candelabra. All is set out on a pristine white linen cloth.

ABOVE RIGHT On Long Island, Vicente Wolf likes to set his picnics in the dappled shade of a cherry tree.
OPPOSITE The theme is pink and Asian: a Japanese chair sits by a piece of fabric found in India and palm leaves act as mats, a bright background for metallic plates from Borneo. All are arranged round a centerpiece found in Burma of Asian lacquer adorned with bright pink blooms.

occasions

EVERYWHERE IN THE WORLD, a feast denotes a celebration, an exceptional and special occasion—a good party, in other words. All special occasions are feasts in one way or another, and demand a particular and exceptional level of attention when it comes to the organization of such events.

A special occasion should be unforgettable in several ways—there should be enough to eat and drink, it should be a treat for the eye, and it should leave every guest feeling happy that they were present. Although some occasions will be formal events set out on traditional lines—perhaps a dinner at table complete with flowers, candelabra and damask napery—others are more informal and might range from a picnic to a buffet party in a barn. Whatever the theme or reason for the event, all special occasions are times to splash out a bit, or even go over the top—they are times when an extravagance of gesture, an element of showmanship, can be most appropriate, and nowhere is this more true than where the decoration of the table and the surrounding area is concerned.

These are the times to take the opportunity to show off your best possessions—china, glass, food and flowers—and to do it in a generous way, to have enough of everything so that guests feel at ease and pampered.

For that is the great treat of a special occasion—that it is a chance to share the moment with others, to make them feel welcome, and that it is for them that you have devised an event that delights and pleases. After all, what would a party be without your guests?

OPPOSITE Nathan Turner creates a very simple, but stylish background to a Mexican feast with fruit-laden branches of oranges arranged in a tall stone urn. PREVIOUS PAGES Preston Bailey knows how to give a party. He has created a table of glittering proportions with sumptuous flowers and layers of intricately conceived decorations.

entertaining family and friends

Historically, social life has revolved around the shared crust and that almost atavistic need is still, thankfully, with us today.

Anyone who enjoys cooking and setting a table likes to entertain their family and friends—it is fun, and it is even more so when you have something to celebrate. The main thing is to keep it simple. Of course first of all there is the food—for Belgian designer, and excellent cook, Agnès Emery, the menu is the most important thing: "Once I have decided on that, then I try to find each plate and each bowl that '*mettre en valeur*' with the food." As she says, "I come from a family where a meal is a feast and a feast, a meal." And Keith Johnson stresses that it is simple but very high-quality ingredients that work the best.

All our creative table setters emphasize the importance of the table looking good, but Sally Sirkin Lewis points out that the added advantage of an imaginatively set table is that it encourages conversation between the guests.

Lighting is extremely important—and it should be low, soft, flattering lighting, achieved through candles alone, or judicious ambient electric lighting—always on a dimmer—combined with candlelight. Comfortable chairs and good music are important, as are flowers that do not restrict the view across the table. And although the ideal number of guests varies from pundit to pundit—no more than eight or possibly ten, says Johnny Roxburgh; up to twenty argues Peri Wolfman—one thing they are all agreed on is that whatever the numbers, giving pleasure to your guests is far and away the most important thing.

BELOW Peri Wolfman likes to make use of natural elements as decoration: flowering plants in simple containers, wine cooled in metal buckets and stones from the beach set at regular intervals down the table create an interesting and hospitable table.

RIGHT Unsurprisingly, the setting of Louise Nason's dinner table is designed to show off chocolate at its best; on her wooden table dark woven mats have replaced pale cloths as they show fewer marks and do not compete with the food, and simple white plates are used to show off the chocolate confections.

BELOW LEFT When it comes to the dessert course, as an alternative to metal cutlery Louise prefers to use wooden tongs for praline and spoons of bone or tortoiseshell which work texturally with the puddings. OPPOSITE Other details—traditional wine glasses, and low bowls of flowers and foliage in contrasting colours—make for a relaxed and welcoming table.

JUST DESSERTS Louise Nason is the owner of Melt, London's most delectable chocolate emporium, where the scent of the chocolates being made in the open kitchen of the shop wafts through the air, tempting many a hungry customer.

Not unnaturally, the dessert course at Louise Nason's suppers is eagerly awaited, and she likes to dress the table accordingly, often differently from the preceding courses and in a way that complements the usually chocolatey dessert. For example, she likes to use dark cutlery rather than light: "People underestimate cutlery; I found these tortoise shell and bone spoons which look wonderful with dark puddings, and have a totally different feel in the mouth, which works well with the chocolate."

She uses flowers cleverly and thoughtfully, too. "Flowers are very important; people tend to look down at a table so low flowers are better; and even better are low flowers from the garden so that they are loose and free." She avoids very tall arrangements for obvious reasons, but sometimes has three different vases—a tall central one to give impact when people come in to the room but which is then removed, and two neighboring low vases which stay on the table throughout the meal.

She prefers to use mats rather than tablecloths—"they don't seem to get wrecked so easily"—and likes them to be made from natural materials so that they don't compete with the food. She is, in fact, and in a very cheerful way, a stickler for detail, not just where her beloved chocolate is concerned, and she likes to create an impact as guests come into the room. "If you tick people's boxes visually, then giving them a better meal is almost easier. If it looks fantastic they think it will taste fantastic too."

"If it looks fantastic they think it will taste fantastic too."

THANKSGIVING Alison Price is an author and a cook as well as a private caterer and party designer; her skills are legendary: she is known for her delicious food, subtle and beautiful settings and the total attention that she gives to the tiniest detail of every event.

Whatever the occasion—whether it is a specific celebration or just an enjoyable dinner—the first thing Alison Price does—even before she decides how the table will be dressed, or what food will be served—is to think about the season in which the event will take place. That becomes her starting point for how she treats the whole event. "I always do that—in a sense, it is more important than anything else; once you have thought about the season, then what to eat, and how to show it at its best, comes naturally."

This approach was particularly important when designing something as specific as a Thanksgiving Dinner! "For Thanksgiving, as for other autumn festivals, I would always use the colors of autumn for the flowers on the table, the decorations behind, even the colors of the candleholders.

"If you are setting a table for something like Thanksgiving, I think that it is important to take into account what the event that you are celebrating actually is and to think about its history—why it evolved and so on. In 1621, not only were the Pilgrims celebrating their first harvest, but they also wanted to demonstrate their gratitude to the native Indians who had shown them how to find new foods—things like corn, squash and the wild turkeys in the area. I had found some pressed glass molds of turkeys so I used them for the soup and I had some baking molds that were shaped like ears of corn so we made cornbread; and then I designed a backdrop using some wonderful ceramic pumpkins and gourds, mixed with small candles in autumn-tinted glasses.'

Extending the table design into the immediate surroundings is something Alison often tries to do —"A table can too easily look cluttered, and so

if there is somewhere else in the room that you can build up a display, it has the added advantage of extending the theme beyond the confines of the table itself."

As far as the details go, she prefers small candles rather than tall, and she loves to use flowers, but ones that are "low and interesting." "I have a lovely collection of antique glass inkwells, for example, and I set them along the length of the table with a single flower or even a sprig of mint in each."

The fact is that Alison always works hard, however informal the dinner—"If you are going to ask friends round, I do feel that you have to make an effort, and the fact is that not only do people really appreciate it but it sets the tone for the evening, making them feel pleased to have been invited."

LEFT The marble-topped sideboard is the setting for a fabulous cornucopia of autumn fruits and flowers: the soaring floral pyramid actually includes, as well as a range of rich autumnal colored flowers, vegetables such as Indian corn, artichokes and cabbages.
RIGHT But all is not as it at first appears: the harvest of autumn fruits on the sideboard—apples, pears, gourds, squashes and pumpkins—is in fact a collection of sturdy, washable hand-crafted and glazed ceramics, made by British company Penkridge Ceramics. Scattered among the autumnal bounty are clusters of candles in golden glazed containers.

"If there is somewhere else in the room that you can build up a display, it has the added advantage of extending the theme beyond the confines of the table itself."

formal dinner parties

The formal feast has always been a part of cultural experience, both in the East and in the West. Many an official function has centered around an evening of fine formal dining with its attendant ceremonies.

In Europe and America, the height of popularity of the formal dinner party was probably the late 19th century, when to give and attend such an occasion was for many the pinnacle of social ambition. Organized like a military campaign, the etiquette involved everything from the issuing and acceptance of invitations, the appropriate dress code (bare shoulders for ladies with elbow-length buttoned gloves) to the rules governing the procession into dinner (ladies would be escorted into the room by a gentleman designated by the hostess). Failure to know such seemingly basic facts such as which of the plethora of cutlery to use or when to turn to your neighbor for conversation were noted. The table itself during this period was a sight to behold—a glittering expanse which included sometimes several centerpieces of a giddying opulence, along with silver, porcelain and, of course flowers, wherever they could be accommodated.

Things are somewhat simpler now, but as art expert and journalist Meredith Etherington-Smith observes, the formal dinner table can still be viewed as a production—the table as the stage, the place settings the props and sets, and the diners the actors.

So it is that most people approach a formal dinner party with a wish to make the event as magical, as special and as glamorous as possible. This is the moment for bringing out your very best china, silver and glass. It is when the food will entice, the surroundings enchant, the guests amuse each other and, even more importantly, enjoy themselves.

"I prefer to stick to clean, uncluttered lines."

OPPOSITE In a monochrome design, Sally Sirkin Lewis's large, variously striped and comfortably upholstered dining chairs are ranged around a glass-topped table set with a number of elements brought together by color—almost exclusively black and white—and a strong sense of order.

LEFT A story of texture: a square red lacquer tray is the background for a black rectangular plate, and a black sake bottle is used as a miniature vase. The fork is of mother-of-pearl, and the napkin ring of onyx.
BELOW Black linen mesh mats form the frame for plates and dishes decorated with waves and dots, and designed by Sally. The glasses are black, as are the linen napkins and the handles of the knives and forks; a subtle contrast is introduced in the mother-of-pearl napkin rings.

SLEEK MODERNISM
Formal comes in several guises—it can be contemporary, and it can be classical: Sally Sirkin Lewis illustrates a graceful interpretation of the former aspect of the genre.

Sally Sirkin Lewis is an American doyenne of design. Based on the West Coast, she is known not only for her sleek contemporary interior design, but also for her textiles, furniture and tableware. A polymath, indeed.

"Basically I'm a contemporary designer and I incorporate all periods into that field; that goes for tables as well as whole rooms! I don't like fussy design in china, silver or tableware and I prefer to stick to clean, uncluttered lines."

"My tables echo that—they are clean in line. I hate short tablecloths—the only tablecloths I have ever owned are full-length ones which I use to hide ungainly table legs—they are particularly useful on square tables; I prefer the look of a glass tabletop set with smart-looking mats and runners."

Crisp clean china is what Sally prefers, but not pure white—"I don't like white at all; ivory is much better, so everything that I buy is a variation on that." To decorate the table she likes old and unusual antiques and flowers, but only white blooms, and never, ever arranged. "I have never used a florist in my life—flowers should be natural."

She lights the table in various ways with subtle, well-considered care. "I like very specific spot lighting on the table, which I effect with dimmers; it's nice to highlight the diners; I also like lighting on the back of the chairs, as well as focused on the center of the table."

RIGHT Ebba Lopez likes to set a Provençal buffet lunch on the terrace, under the shady eaves of her farmhouse. It is not an elaborate meal; it is a come and come-again feast, with terracotta pots containing olives, small *saucisses* and dappled quails' eggs.

buffet parties

A buffet is, by its very stand-up and help-yourself nature, a less formal arrangement than many other eating occasions, and it is also an opportunity for some glamorous decoration.

The idea of a buffet party derives from 18th-century France when food first began to be arranged on the sideboard or buffet from which guests would help themselves, then take their food to a table to eat; the practice then spread through Europe and beyond, becoming established by the second half of the 19th century. This is a mode of eating that is still emulated at some large houses in the country where, at weekends, the breakfast is arranged in this rather convenient, help-yourself, manner.

The modern buffet party draws on this historical precedent, and today's buffet lunch or dinner is a clever and convenient way of entertaining more people than you can comfortably seat in a conventional dinner arrangement. The buffet table itself, whether it is situated indoors or out, stands out as a central, welcoming eye-catcher, a hub to which all your guests can gravitate.

OPPOSITE On rustic wooden boards generous bunches of local radishes and fresh goats' cheese are laid out, all on a woven runner from Linum and decorated with branches that are home to the local *cagouilles*, that look like miniature white snails. LEFT Carolyn Quartermaine sets out a help-yourself breakfast on her sunny roof terrace, using a palette of cool blues and yellows— colored glass and bowls, white cloth and floating blue mats, all against the background of a stone wall.

LEFT A buffet arrangement, whether set for drinks or a more elaborate occasion, should always look welcoming and inviting, and color is an effective way to achieve these aims. Bright flowers and fruits, shades of blue glass and multi-coloured textiles, all invite the guest to come and enjoy the pleasures of the table. OPPOSITE Sleek and ordered is Rumi Verjee's party buffet: ranged along a long high table are square wooden trays, interspersed with gold serving dishes, holding clear and red-bowled glasses the colour of which is echoed by the group of slim, tall, red vases and the Champagne bucket, which is of thick, ridged rubber.

There is an art to giving a successful buffet dinner, and it is, as always, to do with planning. In an intimate setting, Rumi Verjee, chairman of Thomas Goode, in his very stylish, very spare house in London, arranges buffet parties with a military precision, setting out the wherewithal for the buffet on a back-lit surface, with every element very much part of a stylized master plan.

Johnny Roxburgh, of the London-based party event company The Admirable Crichton, starts with a word of sound advice: if it is a very large party, never have more than one course actually on display on the buffet—in other words, set out everything that is going to be served from that table. It is difficult to ask people to visit a buffet twice (although of course they can always help themselves to more of the original!), and it is tricky to remove serving dishes and replace them with others. Better, he feels, to have everything displayed at once with perhaps some food nearer the back, or—if there are seated tables for everyone—to serve one course at the table.

OPPOSITE In the studio in the garden of Tricia Foley's Long Island house, a buffet party is set out, arranged with logic as well as mathematical precision. On the far left of the table the glasses are stood, as well as refreshing bottles of wine; thus fortified, guests can progress along the table to the food beyond.

LEFT Behind the neatly folded napkins and the cutlery box filled with the requisite utensils, the large white dinner plates, designed by Jasper Conran for Wedgwood, are presented in an expanding metal concertina rack, a device both eminently practical in its ease of access and pleasant to look at with its graphic outline.
BELOW Tricia Foley collects creamware both old and new, and many of her pieces are brought into play when she sets out the food for a large party such as this one.

A PERFECTLY PLANNED GATHERING Tricia Foley, an American designer with a long pedigree who is currently working with Wedgwood, has always been a particular whiz with tableware.

Tricia Foley loves china and has long collected it in all its forms—just as long as it is white, or possibly cream. She loves to use her collected ware whenever she can, which more often than not is when she is throwing a buffet party—a mode of entertaining well-suited to having a cupboard full of lovely china, and a lot of friends!

On the grounds of her home on Long Island is a separate studio—this is an ideal space for the giving of large parties, and it is here that she holds her frequent and always well-appointed buffet lunches and suppers.

"In the studio, I have a long stainless steel table—its length makes it just perfect for a buffet because it means that I can put everything that will be needed throughout the evening onto the same table at the same time, instead of having to use different, smaller tables."

While this long table is used solely for serving, sometimes she sets out another table which people can move on to from the buffet table, so that they can sit while they eat, and sometimes not—depending on the numbers at the party. The joy of this arrangement is its flexibility.

On the main buffet table, the components of the meal are not arranged in just any fashion—far from it; Tricia has a

"It's the sense of occasion that I like to have."

ABOVE LEFT In her studio,
which is separate from the
house, Tricia Foley arranges
various party eating options,
from the walk-about party to
the option of having a buffet
set out on a serving table.
ABOVE RIGHT Occasionally
she will set up another table
ready set where the diners
can sit and eat.
OPPOSITE The plates
shown here are one of
Wedgwood's classical white
designs, and the decorative
touches are deliberately
kept simple—small cups of
buttonhole roses and
country blossom.

tried-and-tested method for organizing a really good buffet: "I always work from the left of the table and divide it into imaginary bays: first, I set up the bar—open bottles and glasses of various shapes—on the left hand side of the table so that everyone can help themselves at once to a drink. Next I arrange the place settings all together, using my white Jasper Conran Wedgwood plates in a metal concertina plate rack at the back of the table, and mixing other new and old white and cream ware together. Next, I arrange all the main dishes of food in a group, and at the far right-hand end of the table I set out the dessert, with more plates and the right flatware."

Lighting at a dinner is very important. In the dining room of her house she has no electricity, relying instead on a candle-hung chandelier as well as candles in sconces and on the table. "In my studio, there is electricity and for a buffet I often use two very dramatic, angled lamps at the back of the table, with candles everywhere else in the room. For decoration, I like to use the same simple, broad strokes that I use on the rest of the table—perhaps one big arrangement of flowers, glass cylinders with flowers and branches from the garden, or else simple pots of flowering bulbs. It's the sense of occasion that I like to have, and I think that when the table is arranged and set out like this, people respond to the whole concept, and enjoy it all the more."

celebrations

The ultimate meal, in any culture, is the feast and, throughout the history of civilization, from the ancient cultures of the East through Greeks and Roman civilization, social life has always revolved round a repast.

Banquets were held to celebrate anything from a military victory to the raising of a new temple or an important marriage. They were often statements of power and status, and were usually events of drama and spectacle. The food and drink that was served was, of course, extremely important—many are the records of excessive and indulgent jollifications—and there were usually various forms of entertainment as well, with music, song and dance.

We still follow the same pattern quite closely, particularly on such occasions as weddings or birthdays. Festivities are held at special events, landmarks in our lives, as well as for religious and national days. A feast can be large—for hundreds of people—or it can be small—for four or more; but what distinguishes it from other meals and occasions is that it is always a tribute to something in particular, whether personal or public. Extravagance is the watchword of the celebration—not particularly extravagance in providing the most expensive of everything, but in the hospitality, the time and trouble taken. Perhaps generosity would be a better word—a generosity of spirit that manifests itself in a hospitable and welcoming event. A celebratory party is—or should be—unforgettable.

ABOVE LEFT Agnès Emery gives the best parties—particularly for children; when there is so much going on in a table setting, it is wise to keep the china and glass as simple as possible.
OPPOSITE When Johnny Roxburgh of The Admirable Crichton does a Christmas table, there is no mistaking it for anything else: a faux fur throw for a cloth, gilded china and candlesticks reflecting the firelight, and everything be-ribboned, berried and bowed.

GRAND BIRTHDAY BLOWOUT Johnny Roxburgh and Rolline Frewen are the leading creative spirits behind The Admirable Crichton, the British party design company that they founded together 21 years ago.

Rolline is in charge of the delicious food and glamorous drinks, Johnny is the impresario in charge of everything involved in making a fabulous party. Giving a good party is not that difficult—as long as you pay an awful lot of attention to the details. Johnny Roxburgh has a thing or two to say on the details of giving a party, many of which are exemplified in this lavish, amusing and original birthday party staged in the elegant Link Room in the majestic Chiswick House, an 18th-century mansion in West London.

"First of all, it is paramount that you be able to see across the table, either over or, if you have tall decorations, underneath. Candles need to be set high, never at eye level, and I don't think you should ever use votives or tea lights at a large table—too dangerous; better to use battery-operated candles that flicker in a very convincing way."

LEFT A closer look at the splendid Admirable Crichton festive table reveals that both decorative and culinary details are as important as each other; caviar is served in shallow dishes suspended above a deeper bowl of crushed ice and a graphic langoustine salad is presented in a curved mother-of-pearl shell.
OPPOSITE ABOVE The birthday dessert is created—there is no other word—by Rolline Frewen: a white castle with pennants of spun sugar is surrounded by a moat of red berries.
OPPOSITE BELOW Peggy Porschen is the maker—designer really—of these miniature cakes, each one decorated exquisitely like a present, the icing wrought into ribbons and pleats, and painted like tiny caskets.

As for the place settings themselves: "On a large table, acres of cutlery are too much and off-putting to look at. Instead, lay the table for two courses and then put out the spoons and forks for dessert when the time comes." The same desire to keep the table clear for decorative devices means that he also dislikes side plates: "A place setting with a charger is much better with the bread kept, *à la française*, on one side of the plate. It is nice to have individual salt and pepper servings at every setting; they needn't be in traditional cellars—use whatever looks nice—and you don't need a salt spoon."

Napkins are another area where Johnny holds strong views, and he has some specific recommendations: "They should be 24in (60cm) square, rolled or folded simply, and my personal preference is for lavish, hem-stitched linen; I loathe slippery, colored viscose napkins. You need something clean and soft; a nice touch is to spray them with a lavender-scented linen spray beforehand. A particularly luxurious touch would be to change the napkins for the dessert course."

And what does he think about the tablecloth? "Cloths are great fun and the easiest way to dress up a table; they can be made of almost anything—they don't have to be of silk or some fine material; we sometimes use soft black tablecloths that are very effective." But, he warns, you need to be careful about which color you choose: "The color of the tablecloth should make you feel hungry—certain greens

"A particularly luxurious touch would be to change the napkins for the pudding course."

make you feel sick, and yellow is bad for the complexion. They don't have to be plain colors—a big bold print can look wonderful."

And then there are the flowers: "Nothing too smelly, but other than that, I don't believe there is a single flower that you can't use— even dahlias look wonderful en masse, and carnations used in blocks are also very good. I also like towering glass containers that rise far above the table with flowers arranged at ludicrous angles."

If you are having place cards—essential at a large dinner to avoid confusion when people come to sit down—they should be easy to read and also—so obvious, but so rarely done—they should be written on both sides so that the person on the other side of the table opposite can also see the name of his opposite neighbor.

And above all remember: "It's the people who matter; always have some at the end of a rectangular table so that the guests that end don't feel isolated, and if there is more than one generation mix them up; the old and the young get on very well together."

CREATIVE EXTRAVAGANZA When she gives a children's party, Agnès Emery throws herself into every aspect of design, painting animals and objects that will appeal to every child's imagination.

Agnès Emery, in artistic mode, "goes for the big, dramatic effect"—her favorite children's party design is based around a roll of stiff black paper (bought from an artists' materials supplier) on which she boldly paints white, graphic, almost magical animals and other designs, as well as each child's name by their place setting. The window she also paints, this time with the paint used to apply notices to store front glass, and using a stippling brush she covers the glass with circular shapes that might be snowflakes or shells. On bright red plates she designed herself, she serves mostly bright red food—mixed with a bit of chocolate of course—like dark fruit-filled jelly, cakes and tarts. A party fit for a prince—and princess.

LEFT In her Brussels house, Agnès Emery often gives parties for children in her mirror-decorated dining room. She has painted the window to look as though snow is falling outside using a stubby-ended decorator's brush to roughly stipple the window with easily removable paint.
ABOVE On the black paper she has painted, with white poster paint, leaping animals, snowflakes and—importantly—the names of the guests.

OPPOSITE The paper for the table could be either black art paper or lining paper; either way it is attached to the table with double-sided tape. The china, deliberately simple, and in a palette of red and white, is above all a foil for the party food—a chocolate hedgehog cake and glistening red berries.

FLORAL FESTIVITIES Preston Bailey is one of the best flower designers in the United States. Although he has lived in New York for many years, he hails from Panama, as evidenced by his distinctive, sweeping floral statements.

Preston Bailey always uses flowers when he entertains at his Manhattan apartment. "As my background is as a florist, of course I think that flowers are essential, and naturally I use flowers on the table at home—they make the table, and they make a party." On these more intimate occasions he doesn't go for the towering elephants and fountains of flowers that bestride his tables at larger—very much larger—parties. "I scale everything down; at home it is all to do with specific areas and working with the dining table; it's about the translation of a floral arrangement."

As a background for flowers, Preston chooses the linen with care. "It's so important—I love real linen and also raw silk, which, although it is expensive, you can use as an overlay on a simpler undercloth; then you can get away with using less. I collect textiles so I like to use different things, depending on the mood of the table." And of course, being a flower designer, he likes to enhance the linen with flowers as well. He covers placemats with rose petals and decorates napkins with flowers too: "It's a good idea, and you can use just one flower—something tough like a cymbidium which won't wilt—and lay it on the napkin. It often then becomes a flower for the hair!"

As for china and glass: "Again it's a question of looking to see what you have and then planning accordingly; I like to mix and match—I don't think that they all have to be of the same family. I like to be playful, to shift things around a bit." And as far as

"Naturally I use flowers on the table at home—they make the table, and make a party."

lighting goes, he loves candlelight—most serious table designers do—both tall ones and tealights or votives, which he likes to group together: "as many as possible, to get a soft glow." He also likes to incorporate more technical alternatives, such as halogen lighting: "It's so advanced now—you can have little blocks of light at the table."

Preston points out that the driving force behind the arrangement should be the table, not the other way around—a useful point to remember. "In a small space, rather than an arrangement of average size, low arrangements work well. Or, on the principle that large pieces of furniture make a small room look larger, they could be very tall; it depends on the length of the table and, most importantly on the height of the ceiling. I like groups of roses very low down and one thing that I do sometimes is to deconstruct some roses, break them into petals, and then, using the petals, and working from the outside, build it back into a rose shape that will fit the size of the container."

His final observation is: "I think I like it simple, but simple is subjective—as far as I'm concerned, any dining table should be festive—and that's the same feeling I have when I do a large party as when I do a small dinner at home."

the components

THE EMPEROR NERO'S FAMOUS DINING ROOM with sprays of scent that wafted over the diners and the revolving, domed ceiling on which the heavens and stars were depicted might not be to everyone's taste or budget, but at least he had a sense of occasion and presented a feast in a way that would bring pleasure to his guests.

How the table looks is a combination of so many elements—a fact which could strike panic into the heart but which actually makes one see how easy it is to set a table that looks really well furnished. When there is such a wide choice of glass, linen, china and crockery available—not to mention extra decoration such as flowers and ornaments—how could any table fail to look good?

Start with the surface, as this is the canvas upon which the dressed table is built: if you are buying a new table, make sure that the table is in a finish that will work with your other pieces of furniture, as few people keep a cloth on a table all day. Wood is the traditional material, and infinite in its variety, but there are so many other surfaces available, often combined, from marble and stone to more modern metal, glass and Perspex. If your table is old but not antique, and possibly a bit battered, you may want to keep it permanently covered. In early paintings showing interiors the table was often covered with a carpet—always a valuable possession; today, a flat weave rug or kelim might play the same role, and this could be covered with a lighter cloth at meal times. The important thing is to make the table look as attractive as possible whenever it is on view.

OPPOSITE Marianne Pellerin creates layers upon layers. On a wooden table top, she contrasts textures: first the tablemats, then the china—decorative-edged rectangular plates graded in size—glasses and cutlery; and, above all, the food. PREVIOUS PAGES The components of any table demand attention and are important—first of all the practical aspects, but also, crucially, the aesthetic aspects. The combination of pleasingly useful objects and decorative flourishes cannot fail to present an harmonious whole.

Perhaps the most important consideration when looking for a table is its size and shape—whether it is round, square, rectangular or 'D'-ended, the important thing is that if you are sharing it with others (which you presumably are) it should be easy to both converse normally and eat without feeling cramped. A table that is too narrow to hold the food, the place setting and the diners comfortably is obviously no good, but equally a table that is so wide that each diner is isolated on his or her own little island is not conducive to a convivial occasion. The rule is that you ought to be able to comfortably talk to the person opposite you as well as those beside you at a normal conversational volume.

As we said earlier, the surfaces from which a table can be made are many and various, from wood, metal or stone to marble, plastic and glass, with a hundred combinations of these and other materials in between. Buy what you like and also what will go with your other pieces of furniture. It might be antique and classical; it might be modern and contemporary. It might stand alone in the center as a "look at me" table, or it might sit quietly at one side waiting to play its role. And, of course, a table can always be improvised when you need to seat extra guests—a board on trestles, perhaps covered with something floor-length and full, can look just as glamorous when dressed with style.

But a chair is a different matter—if uncomfortable, a dining chair can, if not ruin, at the very least mar enjoyment of what would otherwise could be a pleasant social occasion. Whatever the material it is made of—and they are as various and many as tables—the important thing is that it should give enough support and be comfortable enough for you to be able to eat and talk, as well as being able to sit back and relax—a seemingly obvious wish-list, but one that is all too often not fulfiled. Since the 18th century, when the idea of comfort first became important, much thought has

gone into the design of chairs and whether you prefer modern or traditional designs, molded or upholstered, with or without arms, or perhaps a combination of these, it is worth spending time and effort searching for your perfect chair.

ABOVE TOP Contemporary and uncompromising, Rumi Verjee's metal-framed table and chairs are flexible individual units, able to be arranged into different combinations, depending on the occasion. ABOVE LEFT The classical lines of the curved backs on the comfortable padded chairs of Stephanie Stokes work well with her round table—a shape that works for either small or larger meals. ABOVE RIGHT Sleek and Scandinavian—no extras mar the lines of this polished table, furnished with both chairs and a bench, always useful for accommodating varying numbers of diners. OPPOSITE A table for all seasons and occasions, made from old wood, wide enough to carrry dishes of food, expansive place settings with ample room for each diner and a host of decorations and surrounded by informal and comfortable high-backed woven chairs.

tables and chairs

linen

There is little new about the idea of a tablecloth; they were highly prized as early as the Middle Ages in Europe. Table linens were always a highly prized and important part of a trousseau, and could be very expensive. What we know as damask tablecloths were originally woven in Damascus, and were known to be the finest available. Nearly always white and woven with subtle, discreet designs, they are still considered the appropriate covering for a very formal dinner. From the 16th to 19th centuries, several cloths were often layered one on top of the other, the topmost layer removed after each course. It is not such a bad idea today to mark the difference between the main course and dessert.

And the idea of layering is a good one and one that should be used more often. The undercloth might be white—there are basic coverings known as hotel cloths, on which you can build. Many people collect or own small cut-work and embroidered cloths, such as the square tea cloths which were so popular in the last century. These are very pretty but too small to cover the average dining table, so layering the smaller cloths on top of a larger one is a clever way to appreciate the pattern and design of the smaller pieces. For a base some people use a piece of cloth or woven textile that was not originally designed as such—anything from an old patchwork quilt to a piece of furnishing fabric—perhaps a heavy printed velvet or dark damask for the best dramatic effect.

Although a white tablecloth is still the color of choice for a formal dinner, colored and patterned cloths work well for less formal occasions, and can act as an effective canvas for the other elements of the dressed table. Runners, once ubiquitous, had been out of favor for a long time, but of late are once again being sighted on the coolest of tables. Due to their lack of popularity, old white linen and cotton ones can still be quite easily picked up in second-hand shops, and when ironed and starched they look as good as the day they were first made. There are also dramatic new designs in heavy felt in bright colors, flat or pleated into concertina-like folds, or made from untraditional materials such as bamboo, cane or rubber.

ABOVE TOP On a table outside, runners are used horizontally, a smart and contemporary take on the traditional idea of a single strip of fabric runing lengthwise down a table, and a useful device for demarcating each place setting. ABOVE LEFT The linen on this table is used in a combination of scales of pattern—both larger and smaller checks in the same or contrasting colors, as here, add a pleasing variety. Larger checks on the cloth help to make the table seem more expansive, while the daintier check of the napkin is more suited to a smaller piece of fabric. ABOVE RIGHT A flower-strewn cloth is both the background for more colors and decorative objects and a pleasing artwork in its own right. OPPOSITE A napkin embroidered with a delicate black-on-white design in a number of stitch patterns is held by two narrow Indian bracelets instead of a more conventional napkin ring.

ABOVE Napkins can play an important part in the decoration and arrangement of a table; here a bold striped napkin in heavy cotton works well with the chunkiness of the bamboo ring and the handles of the cutlery. BELOW Coordinating cloth, mats and napkins by their color and by the graphic nature of their patterns is fun, particularly when they are used, as here, with the contrasting greens of the glassware and foliage. OPPOSITE PAGE: ABOVE LEFT Layer upon layer of luxury: a glass plate with a gilded rim allows the rich pattern of the cloth to show through, and gold-embossed napkins are tied with a knot of gold cord. ABOVE RIGHT For some, this is the ultimate in napkins, and will grace any style of setting, from the ultra formal to the simple everday table: an over-sized starched white damask napkin with a heavy embroidered monogram. BELOW LEFT Not in fact sold as a napkin, but as a dishcloth, this navy and white checked cloth completely fits the bill. BELOW RIGHT A masterly study in subtle tones, the delicately embroidered white napkin is tied with a silver tassel.

Placemats are another option—some placemats that is: laminated ones depicting chocolate box landscape scenes should be avoided or taken to the local charity shop, but traditional fabric ones can work if they are well-laundered, well-ironed and scrupulously clean. If the mats are patterned, the design should be one that will work with the rest of the table. Like runners, placemats have become a new area to explore for designers—made of rubber, leather, wood, metal, bamboo or cane, mats can add an instant touch of novelty. Have several sets, for they are the quickest way of changing the look of a table. Mats which are not padded or insulated will need another heat-proof mat beneath.

Napkins started small and over the centuries got bigger and bigger—until, in the late medieval period they were, says Diana Visser, in her book *The Rituals of Dinner*, about the size of a bath towel, and used "draped over the eater's left arm." From there they moved around to the eater's front, and by the 19th century they found their way to the lap. It is not considered polite to tie them around the neck, but frankly a very large napkin—which you can still find in antique shops or make for yourself—is so much more pleasurable than a small measly little thing.

Colored napkins are fun and are an essential element of the well-arranged table. Generally speaking, patterns are better when they are geometric, rather than floral or botanical, as a geometric design enhances rather than clashes with the food. Napkins should only be made of natural materials: there is nothing more annoying than a piece of synthetic fabric that slips off your lap, skids across your face and never seems to clean your fingers. Using a pleasantly tactile fabric will set the right note of quality to your table.

china

The plates that we know and use today evolved in shape from the thick slices of bread placed on the medieval dining table laid out before each diner to absorb the juices of the food taken from the communal serving dish. Bread gave way to wood and, in wealthier households, pewter, and by the 16th century earthenware dishes were common, evolving into the flat circular plate that we still use today.

Few people today buy one large service that is used for every meal, both formal and informal. It is more popular to choose at least two designs, perhaps one in porcelain or bone china and one that is more sturdy, perhaps in earthenware or stoneware, that can be used for everyday meals.

Others prefer, rather than buying all the various components of an extended full-scale service, to simply buy several sets of plates and dishes that particularly appeal to them and that can be used according to the place and the occasion. Plates are like cushions—new, different plates, added to an existing service or used on their own can completely alter the look of the table and the occasion, and so it is always worth keeping your eyes open for a pleasing new pattern.

Today of course, the choice of design and material is enormous—almost too great, one sometimes thinks. Although the most commonly found designs are either in some form of earthenware, stoneware or more delicate china, one can also find plates in wood, plastic, metal and glass, in all shapes—not only circular, but square, rectangular, and even triangular. Sizes vary from small bread plates to service plates. Service plates are designed to be used as a background for dinner plates and used as an interesting substitute for a placemat.

Every conceivable design possibility exists. Tableware pieces may be plain, pure white or glazed in a single color, delicate or bright. They may be decorated with bands of contrasting color, or hand-painted in an abstract, geometric or figurative design. Printed decoration is another option—perhaps an all-over multi-colored pattern, or monotone motif. Extra ornament in the form of gold or silver might be freely or sparingly used. The choices are endless, so which route to take?

ABOVE TOP Hand made plates and dishes by ceramicist Anne Stocke painted in swirling abstract designs give a wonderfully individual look to a place setting, particularly against the bright red background of the table. ABOVE LEFT John Pawson's individual and intelligent design of contemporary plate is reversible, with one side showing a conventional shape and the other, shown here, indented to be used as a shallow bowl. ABOVE RIGHT A traditional transfer-printed plate illustrates popular 18th-century views in soft monochrome tones that work perfectly with the burnished silver of the tablecloth and the assorted silver decorations. OPPOSITE These striking, starkly graphic contemporary plates and dishes are designed by Sally Sirkin Lewis and, set against a bold black mat, create an elegant backdrop to fine and formal dining.

ABOVE Stephanie Stokes travels frequently in the East and her Cambodian-inspired table reflects this, with local dishes, rattan plate holders, pewter beer mugs and metal candle holders. BELOW The Belgian designer Maarten van Severen was always interested in working with innovative materials, as shown by his Hybrid cutlery designs—a knife made in zirconian ceramic and a lacquered spoon. They are the perfect accompaniment to the John Pawson pure white bowl. OPPOSITE PAGE: ABOVE LEFT A pleasing contrast in texture arises when a delicate porcelain lidded soup bowl is set on a beaten metal lay plate. ABOVE RIGHT There is nothing nicer that timeless, classically shaped china, cutlery and glass: unpretentious and used with a rough-woven cane mat. BELOW LEFT This setting is very Scandinavian and very cool, with Finnish glasses and Swedish plates contrasting strongly with the heavy ridged mats. BELOW RIGHT A little luxury at teatime, courtesy of Thomas Goode, with an ornate and luxurious gilded Japanese tea set and silver cutlery from Tiffany.

Many people like white china or earthenware, and indeed in shape, design and tone white is surprisingly varied and variable, as well as being infinitely adaptable. At its best, nothing looks more stylish and simple, and paradoxically both classical and contemporary. As in paint colors, there is no such thing as "just" white; the tones vary enormously and it can be very rewarding to collect different items or sets that differ slightly from each other. If you are collecting different sets, it is best to stick to either china or earthenware, as a certain similarity in texture is often more pleasing to the eye.

If your taste tends towards colored or patterned plates, and you want to buy more than one design, it is a good idea to have some sort of connecting theme or link between the different patterns that you choose so you can mix together bowls, dishes and plates at will, by whim. It might be color—an element of pink in every pattern, for example—or it might be a common subject, such as floral or botanical patterns. If your taste is towards the geometric, the basic motif might follow through, albeit in different colors and scale. Mismatched but complementary sets are known as harlequin sets, and are a popular way of building up something unique. Really a form of collecting, the search for the next piece can be extremely enjoyable, as you sort through piles at auctions and car boot sales.

Antique china is enjoying a new popularity and buying a set of 19th- or early 20th-century plates or bowls can be a rewarding way of enjoying antiques in an everyday setting. Look also at cheap and cheerful second-hand china. Whether you prefer plain or patterned, bright or light, consider mixing the old and new; a stack of six plates found in a junk shop or market stall can update your existing cache in an amusing, original and unique way.

glassware

From a simple modern carafe to a delicate 17th-century engraved and blown goblet, glass is beautiful in all its manifestations and you can never have too much. It can be handmade—blown, in an almost magical process—or molded by hand or machine. It can be etched, engraved, cut or pressed. It can be extremely expensive and rare; it can be as cheap as anything and tough into the bargain. The range of price as well as the shapes and patterns—not to mention the colors that can be found—mean that every table can have glassware that works with the other elements on the table.

Although some people like to own an entire set of one pattern with everything from beakers to champagne glasses, others like to find different designs and shapes to be used on different occasions.

Hand or machine-made, there is so much choice and, as with china, there is no need to have only one style or design at the table—indeed glasses offer one of the quickest ways to change the look of a table. Water glasses can be a different pattern from wine glasses and large red wine glasses can be of a different design from smaller white wine glasses. On that note, if you are serving wine and using wine glasses, always remember to lay a water glass as well, so that guests have a choice.

If you are collecting across the glass spectrum, it can be fun to link your purchases by color, for there is enough choice both in old glass and new to build up a really interesting collection. Early glass can be found in a range of rich reds and amethysts (ruby and cranberry) as well as a rich blue, called Bristol, and a range of greens from emerald to grass.

Modern glass can be found in almost any color you care to think of and the combination, even in small doses, adds a warm element to any table, so it is fun to have some even if the majority of your glass collection is clear. Gilded decoration on glass is the ultimate luxury—even a single band gives an air of richness and opulence. Patterned glass has its own group of admirers, and many people collect glasses that are linked by one type of design—perhaps the ubiquitous vine or hop leaves that adorned many 18th- and 19th-century drinking glasses.

ABOVE TOP Using colored glass is a good way to extend a color theme, or even introduce a little color to an otherwise neutral scheme. Colored pressed glass is part of the American craft tradition and comes in many, many shades and designs. ABOVE LEFT Classical shapes with relatively simple decoration in glass old and new work well in this subdued table scheme of grisaille tones. ABOVE RIGHT Antique hock glasses with the traditional round bowls and green stems are both distinctive and beautiful, and echo wonderfully both the shape and color of the acid-green budded roses grouped together in the center of the table. OPPOSITE The perfect glasses for a formal dinner at Rumi Verjee's house—these etched, cut and gilded hand-blown glasses from Moser are just perfect examples of the glass designer's art.

ABOVE Tricia Foley clusters short-stemmed, clear glass flutes together at her buffet table. Not only do they make a pleasing group in combination like this, they are a very practical shape for a party as they are easy to hold in the hand. BELOW For her courtyard lunch, Agnès Emery uses simple glass decanters, finished with ethereal hand-blown glass stoppers made for her in Morocco, their organic shapes resembling the flowering plants and stems beyond. OPPOSITE: ABOVE LEFT These rose-pink rimmed semi-opaque glasses are in sharp contrast to the rough stone table and complement the deep red blooms cut low in a tumbler. ABOVE RIGHT The tones of the delicate lilac glass are reinforced by the lilac of the table napkins. BELOW LEFT The array of festive glasses seems even greater when reflected in the mirrored table created by The Admirable Crichton for a birthday feast. BELOW RIGHT On a table of monochrome tones and little color, wine goblets banded in silver—a smart alternative to the more usual gold—fit in with the overall mood, which is cool, clear and crisp.

The shape of a glass is all-important and what you choose is very much due to individual preference as well as any practical considerations. Glass has always been, and still is, a material that inspires inventiveness in the designer glassmaker, and both contemporary and traditional shapes sometimes soar to flights of ethereal, sculptural fancy. Some people like a large chunky goblet, others a finer, angled shape, akin to a bud vase. Traditionally, a tulip shape was used for wine but many prefer a rounded shape with heavy base—all have their merits and advantages; the decision is based on personal taste. If you have interesting glassware take the opportunity to show it off: use individual pieces for other things as well as holding liquid; flowers for instance. Individual bouquets set in front of each plate are a very welcoming personal touch, or add a number of tea lights, arranged together in the centre of the table.

Glass is fragile—obvious to say, but it does bear being treated with respect, especially during the cleaning process, as this is when most damage occurs. No hand-made glass, cut glass or antique glass should be washed in dishwashers as the detergent is too strong and can not only dim the surface of the glass but also have an abrasive effect on the cut designs. Old glass, particularly lead crystal, is easily scratched—a counsel of perfection is to wash it by hand in a plastic bowl rather than in a metal or enamel sink. Good glasses should always be dried with a traditional linen glass cloth that will polish the glass without harming it.

Glass, whether it is old or new, should always be stored with the bowl upwards, not turned upside down as so many people do to stop dust entering; the rim is the most fragile part of the glass and storing them upside down will inevitably cause chipping.

cutlery

The familiar cutlery shapes we see on our dining tables today have quite specific and practical origins. A knife was originally a hunting weapon, a fork is a sophistication of the pointed knife and a spoon is a bowl attached to an elongated handle. Originally the hunting knife, a substantial and by necessity very sharp tool, was used to cut the food while a smaller knife was used to hold the food firmly in place. It was this lesser instrument that evolved into a two-pronged and then a three-pronged piece—the fork. The knife itself has reduced in size over the years—originally far larger than the accompanying fork, as an indication of its former importance to the owner, it is today roughly the same size. These two

pieces, added to the always useful round-bowled spoon—which was used for serving as well an an individual's use—meant that by the 18th century between these three implements all food could be managed, enjoyed and eaten in what we would describe as a polite, as well as a practical, way. There have been periods since then—during the late 19th and early 20th centuries especially—when new implements were produced to supposedly deal better with particular foods and dishes, such as flat-bladed fish knives and forks to fillet the fish and pointed grapefruit spoons to cut

the citrus flesh—but, by and large, we have now returned to the original designs, so well suited to their purpose.

People can be quite obsessive about their choice of cutlery—particularly about the pattern if they have opted for a traditional one. Many of the patterns we like today were first created in the 17th and 18th centuries, their designs stemming directly from the motifs of the architecture and decoration of the time; new cutlery in these traditional patterns is still widely made and easy to find, but it is also not difficult to track down old pieces—often sold in mixed bundles in antique shops and markets and usually very good value, all the more so if you do not mind having pieces from

different periods though all of the same design. When combining pieces in this way try to consider the material of the blade and the handle—on both an aesthetic and practical level, it helps to have some sort of continuity.

ABOVE TOP Eclectic is what Keith Johnson and Glen Senk do, and for that they require beautifully designed cutlery that works equally well with both old and new styles of china and glass ware. ABOVE LEFT As an accompaniment to the chocolate tart, this bone spoon is not only the perfect complementary color, but is also an interesting textural contrast, with a completely different feel from metal. ABOVE RIGHT A contemporary set of cutlery is the perfect partner for a contemporary setting by Voon Wong using his innovative china tableware designs; the fluid lines of the ultra-slim knife, fork and spoon have a spare elegance. OPPOSITE Luxury and opulence are paramount in this set of plated cutlery; Asian in style, each individual place setting comes with its own raw silk storage pouch to protect these beautiful pieces when they are not being used.

ABOVE At an informal meal, outdoors in California, what could be more appropriate than a set of prettily decorated ceramic-handled cutlery. BELOW Bone and ivory handles were once a traditional design for cutlery handles; most modern versions are made from plastic or resin. OPPOSITE Tricia Foley collects old knives, forks and spoons of different designs and mixes them all together for her buffet parties. They form a delightful composition of contrasts displayed in a row like this.

First and foremost, of course, the knife, fork and spoon should do the job for which they were designed, which is not quite as obvious as it seems, because sometimes, and particularly with new designs, the shape appears to be designed more for its looks than its function. However impressive cutlery looks laid on the table, it will be immensely irritating if you simply cannot eat with it. All three pieces should be of a good weight and feel satisfying in the hand, the handle should be easy to grasp and the blade of the knife should cut easily, while being broad enough to push the food onto the fork. The bowl of the spoon should be deep enough, and the fork should have tines which are well spaced and sharp enough to spear the food.

There is, today, a wide choice of materials for knives and forks, most knife blades being made in stainless steel, for practical reasons. Many people search out old knives with ordinary steel blades, which, although they need careful and rather laborious cleaning, have a charm of their own. Handles can be made of metal—sterling or plated silver, gilded, stainless steel or iron—but traditionally, handles were made of ceramic, wood, bone or ivory, the last of which now is reproduced in a composite material which imitates the original color and texture. You can find designs in bamboo (real and imitation), glass, Perspex and plastic, the latter colored and patterned, clear and opaque, and embellished with extra decoration. And like chess men, handles can now be molded into every sort of shape from Egyptian gods to apostles and knights.

Look after your cutlery; if it is old, always wash it by hand and dry the knives particularly carefully. Even if it is dishwasher proof, it is a good idea to stack the knives handle up so that the water drips down onto the blade rather than vice versa.

Candles on and around the dining table say that an effort has been made, that your guests are expected and welcomed. Even if you use electric lighting, candles are the traditional lighting when food is served, particularly for festivities and feasts. And for good reason: not only do they illuminate the table, but candlelight also flatters the dishes on the table, and the faces around it. The choice and variety of candles is huge, from gigantic pillar candles which can be placed in glass hurricane lamps and storm lanterns, to little nightlights which can be arranged in front of each place or grouped together down the length of the table—perhaps on a long wooden board, surrounded by flower petals or leaves

Traditional candlesticks or branched candelabra always achieve a good effect, and many people collect different pairs, or even single sticks, to make a group of varying shapes and sizes. The only proviso is that the sticks should be high enough, or low enough, to let people see each other on opposite sides of the table. On a long table, it is a good idea to vary the height of the lighting by combining any taller candlesticks or candelabra with groups of tealights at table level, singly in front of place settings or grouped together in blocks along the table. Look also for unusual free-standing candles

which are now made in a variety of sizes, shapes and finishes, and can be used as an integral part of the overall

decorative scheme. As far as the color of the candle goes, traditionalists prefer cream (rather than white) candles in a cylinder rather than tapered shape. But colored candles have a place, particularly in a color-based scheme, and silver and gold can look very dramatic on a formal table. Scented candles should never be used at the table—the conflict of artificial and food smells is not a good idea.

Electric light around the dining table, although sometimes practical, particularly before and after the meal, should be used with circumspection and care—particularly central overhead lights. While ambient lighting—table lamps and dimmed down lighters—can add depth and texture to a setting, a single overhead light that illuminates indiscriminately is to be avoided—it flatters neither dishes nor diner.

ABOVE TOP As well as cutlery and china, architect and designer John Pawson has designed some beautiful decorative pieces for the table including these simple classic candle holders that follow the principle of storm lanterns with their clear glass funnels. ABOVE RIGHT In an elegantly appointed dining room, with the table beautifully set for a fine dining experience, nothing looks better than a full-blown crystal drop chandelier hung from the ceiling, augmented with candles on the table itself. ABOVE LEFT François Gilles is fond of the decoration of the 1950s, and in homage has hung, in his dining room, colored glass pendant lights low over the table. OPPOSITE On a table decorated in soft shades of silver and gray, single, tall candles set in low square silver bases, are complemented by clusters of gilded glasses holding tealights.

lighting

flowers

Throughout this book there are some wonderfully creative ideas for using flowers at the table, from the simplest scheme to the most elaborate. Here we give some general guidelines for how best to choose the right plants and flowers.

By the mid 19th century, fresh flowers were generally considered essential on the dining table, as part of the Victorian taste for ornate decoration. They were used in complex and complicated arrangements, often wrought into almost artificial structures, with towering centerpieces and garlands of white smilax and greenery running in deep loops down the sides of the table.

In our own time, although our taste is perhaps not quite as elaborate as that of our predecessors, nearly every hostess likes to use flowers as often as possible—and who wouldn't, given the choice of color and variety that can be found today? "Natural" should always be the watchword, even though the effort taken to achieve this natural look can be sometimes rather unnatural!

First—this is so important that it bears repeating—remember the iron rule that all flower arrangements should be either so high that you can see beneath them across the table, or so low that you can see the diner sitting opposite you over the blooms. The latter solution does not have to mean restricting yourself to small flowers—large flower heads can be cut right back so that no stem is left and they can be displayed at a much lower level.

The decision of whether to have one central arrangement rather than several placed along the length of the table, or indeed what you might call personal posies in front of every place, is one that must be influenced by the complexity and quantity of the food that is to be served. There should be room for both elements, without any sense of overcrowding. Flowers do not need to be expensive—it is the idea of fresh decoration that is appealing, not necessarily the fact that these are all hothouse

blooms, rare and beautiful. Just as some hostesses never have scented candles on a dining table as they detract from the scents of the food, so successful party planners also ban highly scented flowers for the same reasons.

ABOVE TOP Preston Bailey is the American master of imaginative and unusual floral centerpieces, exemplified by this elegant spiral of wired orchid heads backed with sharp acid-green chrysanthemums, studded with pendulous glass drops. ABOVE LEFT Flowers that are traditionally displayed on their original long stems, such as these lilies and roses, take on a completely different look when they are cut right down and arranged in simple glass vases. ABOVE RIGHT On a birthday party table devoted to the art of the decorated cake, even the flowers have been designed to look like an oversized cupcake. OPPOSITE Peri Wolfman loves to include flowers on her tables, but only in single colors, and she prefers to use those that are in their natural season rather than forced blooms. She groups them together, like these white tulips, in simple funnel-shaped vases of different heights.

ABOVE At Alison Price's Thanksgiving dinner, seasonal flowers and fruit have been carefully designed in suitably festive shapes. BELOW The charm of garden flowers and foliage such as daisies and *Alchemilla mollis* are best appreciated at close quarters as here, where they are displayed in a variety of low and small containers and glasses. OPPOSITE A Moroccan feast is made even more glamorous with an opulent arrangement of flowers, fruit and foliage in the rich colors of the table setting.

Central pieces should be arranged so that they are seen to advantage from every angle; individual bouquets can be less formal—small flowers, cut down and arranged in anything from egg cups to miniature vases or bottles, and every sort of glass from decorative tea glasses, sherry or shot glasses to brandy balloons or colored liqueur glasses. Cottage garden flowers such as cornflowers, sweet peas and lilies-of-the valley are particularly appealing displayed in this way.

If you are arranging more than one group on the table, there is merit in repeating the theme precisely along the table: it might be a line of simple square glass vases, each one crammed with short-stemmed white tulips, or two or three narrow-necked decanters, each one containing just one or two perfect long-stemmed roses. And not only flowers can be used as fresh decoration: one successful scheme uses bunches of fresh herbs—fennel, rosemary, flat-leaf parsley and mint, for example—gathered into mixed bunches and arranged in simple, small, straight-sided glass vases, the impact coming from the differing shades of greens and variety of herby foliage.

Instead of cut flowers, small flowering plants can be a very pretty way to decorate the table—and they can be enjoyed later, or planted out in a windowbox or flowerbed. Delicate-looking plants, like pansies, pinks and miniature iris, can be decanted into small terracotta flower pots or packed into straight-sided glass jars, miniature metal milk pails or perhaps little Chinese ornamental ceramic bowls, perhaps with some moss packed around the stalks of the plant.

Think of the table as a whole and contrast the chosen flowers and their containers with the table surface and the type of tablecloth used—chunky metal boxes on a lace tablecloth, perhaps, or delicate glass and china on a contemporary background.

other
decorations

Since medieval times, the dining table has been the setting for great decorative displays, which became more and more ambitious, culminating in the spectacles in 16th-century Renaissance Italy when at court banquets, according to Roy Strong's illuminating book *Feast*, sugar was mixed with other ingredients, fashioned into almost life-size architectural fantasies of remarkable complexity, painted and gilded, then set in front of the astonished guests. The fashion spread across Europe, albeit in sometimes more modest form, and no grand table was thought to be complete

without an extravaganza of decoration. Our tables today are in many ways far simpler, which is not the same as saying

that they are dressed without thought. The impetus is still there but on the whole, the aim is to make the diners feel comfortable and to please them with our choice of decorative, interesting objects rather than overwhelm them with our efforts. Natural decoration always works well—a grouping of shells perhaps or coloured stones or pebbles. Following the 18th-century tradition, the table acts as a good setting for small ceramic figurines, or groups of porcelain or terracotta birds— anything in fact that you might otherwise display on a mantelpiece or small sideboard can be brought to the dining table. Delicate pieces of silver, miniature obelisks and architectural forms—anything can be used as long as it is in scale and it does not impede either the serving of food, or the ease with which guests can talk with others across the table.

Whimsy is acceptable as long as it is not overdone—the colored paper birds and butterflies that can be found in paper goods stores, and some of the decorations made to be attached to the branches of a Christmas tree but which are equally pretty on other occasions, such as gilded papier mâché partridges and peacocks, can be pretty and interesting incorporated into a table design. Napkins can be rolled and

fastened with colored ribbon, string or twine, or a cheap and cheerful bracelet from a shop in Chinatown. The only thing to remember is that if you are doing a themed table don't overload the references—enough is always enough.

ABOVE TOP The gift of being able to arrange seemingly disparate decorative objects into a pleasing whole is one that is invaluable when it comes to putting together an elaborate setting made up of many elements; Diane Fisher-Martinson definitely has this skill. ABOVE LEFT Alison Price likes to develop a theme to its ultimate conclusion; on her seaside dinner table, everything from the star fish down to the shell salt holder is inspired by the sea. ABOVE RIGHT François Gilles uses color and simple objects as a striking form of table decoration, as here where the red-toned apples on the fruit stand are the link between the table surface and the hand-made ceramics. OPPOSITE Rumi Verjee loves the unexpected and unusual—such as these intricate metal pagoda-shaped napkin rings and dark wooden mats, linked with rows of metal rivets.

DESIGNERS who feature in this book

Abigail Ahern
Atelier Abigail Ahern
137 Upper Street
London N1 1QP, UK
Tel: +44 (0) 20 7354 8181
www.atelierabigailahern.com

Preston Bailey
147 West 25th Street, 11th Floor
New York, NY 10001
Tel: 212 741 9300
www.prestonbailey.com

Kristof & Stefan Boxy
Boxy's
Mortelstraat 91
9831 Deurle
Belgium
Tel: +32 9 385 8733
www.boxys.be

Agnès Emery
Emery & Cie
27 rue d l'Hopital
1000 Brussels
Belgium
Tel: +32 2 513 5892
www.emeryetcie.com

Tricia Foley
tricia@triciafoley.com
www.wedgwood.com

François Gilles
IPL Interiors
Studio 4a
75-81 Burnaby Street
London SW10 0NS, UK

Delphine Krakoff
Pamplemousse Design Inc
157 East 61st Street
New York, NY 10021
Tel: 212 980 2033
delphine@
pamplemoussedesign.com

Beatrice Lafontaine
When Objects Work
Tel: +32 50 61 33 54
www.whenobjectswork.be

Ebba Lopez
Linum France SAS
ZAC due Tourail
Coustellet
84660 Maubec
France
Tel: +33 490 76 34 00
www.linum-france.com

Louise Nason
Melt Chocolates
59 Ledbury Road
London W11 2AA, UK
Tel: +44 (0) 20 7727 5030
www.meltchocolates.com

Gilles & Marianne Pellerin
Collection Privée
9 rue des Etat-Unis
06400 Cannes
France
Tel: +33 4 97 06 94 94
www.collection-privee.com

Alison Price
Alison Price & Company
Norfolk House, 5a Cranmer Road
London SW9 6EJ, UK
Tel: +44 (0) 20 7840 7640
www.alisonprice.co.uk

Carolyn Quartermaine
Carolyn Quartermaine Studio
7 Philbeach Gardens
London SW5 9EY, UK
Tel: +44 (0) 20 7373 4492
www.carolynquartermaine.com

Johnny Roxburgh
Admirable Crichton
Unit 5, Camberwell Trading Estate
Denmark Road
London SE5 9LB, UK
Tel: +44 (0) 20 7326 3800
www.admirable-crichton.co.uk

John Saladino
200 Lexington Avenue
New York, NY 10016
Tel: 212 684 6805
www.saladinostyle.com

Glen Senk and Keith Johnson
Anthropologie
www.anthropologie.com

Nicolette Schouten
Collection Privée
3 rue des Etat-Unis
06400 Cannes
France
Tel: +33 4 93 99 23 23
www.collection-privee.com

Sally Sirkin-Lewis
J Robert Scott
500 North Oak Street
Inglewood, CA 90302
Tel: 877 207 5130
www.jrobertscott.com

Stephanie Stokes
Stephanie Stokes Inc
139 East 57th Street
New York, NY 10022
Tel: 212 756 9922
www.stephaniestokesinc.com

Thomas Goode
19 South Audley Street
London W1K 2BN, UK
Tel: +44 (0)20 7499 2823
www.thomasgoode.com

Nathan Turner
636 Almont Drive
Los Angeles
CA 90069
Tel: 310 275 1209
www.nathanturner.com

Vicente Wolf
Vicente Wolf Associates Inc
333 West 39th Street
New York, NY 10018
Tel: 212 465 0590
www.vicentewolfassociates.com

Voon Wong
VoonBenson
Unit 3d, Burbage House
83 Curtain Road
London EC2A 3BS, UK
Tel: +44 (0) 20 7033 8763
www.voon-benson.com

directory

CHINA AND GLASS

Atelier Abigail Ahern
137 Upper Street
London N1 1QP, UK
Tel: +44 (0) 20 7354 8181
www.atelierabigailahern.com

Baccarat
63 rue Edouard Vaillant
92300 Levallois Perret, France
Tel: +33 820 32 22 22
www.baccarat.com

Chinacraft Ltd
Parke House
130 Barlby Road
London W10 6BW, UK
Tel: +44 (0) 20 7565 5876
www.chinacraft.co.uk

The Crockery Barn
Ashbocking, Ipswich
Suffolk IP6 9JS, UK
Tel: +44 (0) 1473-890123
www.thecrockerybarn.co.uk

The Conran Shop
407 E. 59th Street
New York, NY 10022
Tel: 866 755 9079
www.conranusa.com

Davda
342 Kilburn Lane
London W9 3EF, UK
Tel: +44 (0) 20 8969 3239
www.brickettdavda.com

The Denby Pottery Company
Denby, Derbyshire DE5 8NX, UK
Tel: +44 (0) 1773 740899
www.denbypottery.co.uk

Dibor
20a West Park, Harrrogate
North Yorkshire HG1 1BJ, UK
Tel: +44 (0) 870 0133 666
www.dibor.co.uk

Divertimenti
139-41 Fulham Road
London SW3 6SD, UK
Tel: +44 (0) 20 7581 8065
www.divertimenti.co.uk

Essentially White Limited
1 Ford Place Cottages
Ford Lane, Wrotham Heath
Sevenoaks, Kent TN15 7SE, UK
Tel: +44 (0) 845 404 9505
www.essentiallywhite.co.uk

The General Trading Company
2 Symons Street, Sloane Square
London SW3 2TJ, UK
Tel: +44 (0) 20 7730 0411
www.general-trading.co.uk

Thomas Goode
19 South Audley Street
London W1K 2BN, UK
Tel: +44 (0) 20 7499 2823
www.thomasgoode.com

Marks and Spencer Group plc
Waterside House
35 North Wharf Road
London W2 1NW, UK
Tel: +44 (0) 20 7935 4422
www.marksandspencer.com

Meissen
Buy Meissen
Admiral Vernon Antique Market
141-149 Portobello Road
London W11 2GB, UK
Tel: +44 (0) 7786 243608
www.buymeissen.com

Mulberry Hall
Stonegate, York YO1 8ZW, UK
Tel: +44 (0) 1904 620736
www.mulberryhall.co.uk

Murano Glass
Via Treportina nr. 30
Cavallino-Treporti 30100
Venice, Italy
www.murano-glass-shop.it

OKA Direct
Chene Court, Poundwell Street
Modbury, Devon PL21 0QL, UK
Tel: +44 (0) 870 160 6002
www.okadirect.com

La Porcelaine Blanche
32, Rue de l'Hôtel des Postes
06000 Nice, France
Tel: +33 493 621 125
www.laporcelaineblanche.com

Reject China Shop
183 Brompton Road
London SW3 1NF, UK
Tel: +44 (0) 20 7581 0739

Royal Creamware Fine China
Royal Chintz
Wolrld Wide Shopping Mall Ltd
Chancery Lane, Malton
North Yorkshire YO17 7HW, UK
Tel: +44 (0) 1653 602880
www.royalcreamware.co.uk

Royal Doulton USA
200 Cottontail Lane
Somerset, NJ 08873
Tel: 1 800 682 4462
www.royaldoulton.com

Royal Worcester
Moorestown, NJ 08057
Tel: 1 856 866 2900
www.royalworcester.com

Small Island Trader Ltd
Brockton Hall, Brockton
Stafffordshire ST21 6LY, UK
Tel: +44 (0) 1785 851800
www.smallislandtrader.com

Spode
Church Street, Stoke-on-Trent
Staffordshire ST4 1BX, UK
Tel: +44 (0) 1782 744011
spodeinfo@royalchina.com
www.spode.com

Tableware UK
183 Brompton Road
London SW3 1NF, UK
Tel: +44 (0) 20 7565 5883
www.tableware.uk.com

Josiah Wedgwood & Sons Ltd
Barlaston, Stoke-on-Trent
Staffordshire ST12 9ES, UK
Tel: 1 800 955 1550
www.wedgwood.com

Villeroy & Boch
267 Merton Road
London SW18 5JS, UK
Tel: +44 (0) 20 8871 0011
www.villeroy-boch.com

Voon Benson
Unit 3d, Burbage House
83 Curtain Road
London EC2A 3BS, UK
Tel: +44 (0) 20 7033 8763
www.voon-benson.com

When Objects Work
Tel: +32 50 61 33 54
www.whenobjectswork.com

TABLE LINEN AND FABRIC

Annie's Vintage Costume and Textiles
10 Camden Passage
London N1 8EG, UK
Tel: +44 (0) 20 7359 0796

Antique Designs Ltd
Ash House, Ash House Lane
Little Leigh, Northwich
Cheshire CW8 4RG, UK
Tel: +44 (0) 1606 892822/3
www.antique-designs.co.uk

Jane Churchill
151 Sloane Street
London SW1X 9BX, UK
Tel: +44 (0) 20 7730 9847
www.janechurchill.com

Cologne & Cotton Ltd
74 Regent Street
Royal Leamington Spa
Warwickshire CV32 4NS, UK
Tel: +44 (0) 1926 881485
www.cologneandcotton.net

The Egyptian Cotton Store Ltd
76 Ewhurst Road, Crawley
West Sussex RH11 7HE, UK
Tel: +44 (0) 845 226 0098
www.egyptiancottonstore.com

Givan's Irish Linen
Suite14
Queen Street Chambers
Queen Street
Peterborough PE1 1PA UK
Tel: +44 (0) 1733 562 300
www.givans.co.uk

Judy Greenwood Antiques
657 Fulham Road
London SW6 5PY, UK
Tel: +44 (0) 20 7736 6037
www.judygreenwoodantiques.co.uk

John Lewis
Oxford Street
London W1A 1EX, UK
Tel: +44 (0) 20 7629 7711
www.johnlewis.com

Linum France SAS
ZAC due Tourail
Coustellet
84660 Maubec
France
Tel: +33 490 76 34 00
www.linum-france.com

King of Cotton
Unit 5, The Sandycombe Centre
1/9 Sandycombe Road
Richmond on Thames
Surrey TW9 2EP, UK
Tel: +44 (0) 20 8332 7999
www.kingofcotton.co.uk

Knickerbean
4 Out Northgate Street
Bury St. Edmunds
Suffolk IP33 1JQ, UK
Tel: +44 (0) 1284 704055
www.knickerbean.com

La Maison de Lices
2 Boulevard Louius-blanc
83990 Saint Tropez
France
Tel: +33 4 94 97 64 64
www.la-maison-des-lices.com

Ian Mankin
109 Regents Park Road
London NW1 8UR, UK
Tel: +44 (0) 20 7722 0997
www.ianmankin.com

Jane Sacchi Linens Ltd
Worlds End Studios
132-134 Lots Road
London SW10 0RJ, UK
Tel: +44 (0) 20 7349 7+44 (0) 20
www.janesacchi.com

Tobias and the Angel
68 Whitehart Lane, Barnes
London SW13 0PZ, UK
Tel: +44 (0) 20 8878 8902
www.tobiasandtheangel.com

Volga Linen Company
Unit 1A,
Eastlands Road Industrial Estate
Leiston, Suffolk IP16 4LL, UK
Tel: +44 (0) 1728 635020
www.volgalinen.co.uk

The White Company
Tel: +44 (0) 870 900 9555
www.thewhitecompany.com

The White House
102 Waterford
London SW6 2HA, UK
Tel: +44 (0) 20 7629 3521
www.the-white-house.com

Woods of Harrogate Limited
Prince Albert Row
65/67 Station Parade, Harrogate
North Yorkshire HG1 1ST, UK
Tel: +44 (0) 1423 530111
www.woodsofharrogate.co.uk

PLACEMATS

The Direct Leather Company
Tel: +44 (0) 845 226 0882
www.thedirectleathercompany.co.uk

Jo Downs Glass Design Ltd
Unit 5 Merchants Quay
Pennygillam Industrial Estate
Launceston
Cornwall PL15 7ED, UK
Tel: +44 (0) 1566 779779
www.jodowns.com

Graham and Green
4 Elgin Crescent
London W11 2JA, UK
Tel: +44 (0) 20 7727 4594
www.grahamandgreen.co.uk

Tablewareshop.co.uk
PO Box 29705
London NW3 7NH, UK
Tel: +44 (0) 20 7120 1325
www.tablewareshop.co.uk

CUTLERY

Alessi USA Inc.
155 Spring St., 4th floor
New York, NY 10012
www.alessi.com

Arborio
Maitland House,
Battledown Approach
Cheltenham GL52 6RA, UK
Tel: +44 (0) 845 680 1936
www.arborio.co.uk

David Mellor
4 Sloane Square
London SW1 8EE, UK
Tel: +44 (0) 20 7730 4259
www.davidmellordesign.com

Glazebrook & Co
PO Box 1563
London SW6 3XD, UK
Tel: +44 (0) 20 7731 7135
www.glazebrook.com

Arthur Price
Britannia Way, Lichfield
Staffordshire WS14 9UY, UK
Tel: +44 (0) 1543 257775
www.arthurprice.com

Puiforcat
48 Avenue Gabriel
75008 Paris, France
Tel: +33 (0) 1 45 63 10 10
www.puiforcat.com

William Turner Master Cutlers
Freepost 756
Sheffield S11 8WW, UK
Tel: +44 (0) 114 275 7487
www.williamturnersheffield.com

Viners
Oneida Ltd
P.O. Box 1, Oneida
NY 13421-2899
Tel: 1 888 263 7195
www.oneida.com

Robert Welch
Lower High Street, Chipping Campden
Gloucestershire GL55 6DY, UK
Tel: +44 (0) 1386 840 522
www.welch.co.uk

Studio William Welch Ltd
Goose Hill, Charingworth
Chipping Campden
Gloucestershire GL55 6NU, UK
Tel: +44 (0) 1386 800 000
www.studiowilliamshop.co.uk

ACCESSORIES AND LIGHTING

After Noah
121 Upper Street, London N1 1QP, UK
Tel: +44 (0) 20 7359 4281
www.afternoah.com

Anthropologie
www.anthropologie.com

Atelier Abigail Ahern
137 Upper Street, Islington
London N1 1QP, UK
Tel: +44 (0) 20 7354 8181
www.atelierabigailahern.com

Alfies' Antique Market
13-25 Church Street
London NW8 8DT, UK
Tel: +44 (0) 20 7723 6066
www.alfiesantiques.com

Aram Designs
110 Drury Lane
London WC2B 5SG, UK
Tel: +44 (0) 20 7557 7557
www.aram.co.uk

Artemide
90-92 Great Portland Street
London W1 7JY, UK
Tel: +44 (0) 20 7637 7238
www.artemide.com

Bella Figura
G5 Chelsea Harbour Design Centre
Chelsea Harbour
London SW10 0XE, UK
Tel: +44 (0) 20 7376 4564
www.bella-figura.co.uk

David Canepa Lighting
Dragonworks
Leigh-on-Mendip
Radstock BA3 5QZ, UK
Tel: +44 (0) 1373 813600
www.canepalighting.co.uk

Collection Privée
9 rue des Etat-Unis
06400 Cannes
France
Tel: +33 4 97 06 94 94
www.collection-privee.com

John Cullen Lighting
585 Kings Road
London SW6 2EH, UK
Tel: +44 (0) 20 7371 5400
www.johncullenlighting.co.uk

De le Cuona Ltd
9/10 Osborne Mews
Windsor, Berkshire SL4 3DE, UK
Tel: +44 (0) 1753 830301
www.delecuona.co.uk

Emery & Cie
27 rue d l'Hopital
1000 Brussels
Belgium
Tel: +32 2 513 5892
www.emeryetcie.com

Erco
38 Dover Street
London W1, UK
Tel: +44 (0) 20 7408 0320
www.erco.com

Habitat
196 Tottenham Court Road
London W1P 9LD, UK
Tel: +44 (0) 845 601 0740
www.habitat.net

Ikea USA
Stores nationwide in the
United States
www.ikea.com

The London Lighting Company
135 Fulham Road
London SW3 6RT, UK
Tel: +44 (0) 20 7589 3612
www.londonlighting.co.uk

Mr Light
279 King's Road
London SW3 5EW, UK
Tel: +44 (0) 20 7352 8398
www.mrlight.co.uk

Penkridge Ceramics
Argent Works
Bott Lane
Walsall
West Midlands WS1 2JJ, UK
Tel: +44 (0) 1922 625181
www.penkridgeceramics.co.uk

J Robert Scott
500 North Oak Street
Inglewood, CA 90302
Tel: 877 207 5130
www.jrobertscott.com

SCP
135-39 Curtain Road
London EC2A 3BX, UK
Tel: +44 (0) 20 7739 1869
www.scp.co.uk

Skandium
72 Wigmore Street
London W1H 9DL, UK
Tel: +44 (0) 20 7935 2077
www.skandium.com

Stephanie Stokes Inc
139 East 57th Street
New York, NY 10022
Tel: 212 756 9922
www.stephaniestokesinc.com

Nathan Turner
636 Almont Drive
Los Angeles, CA 90069
Tel: 310 275 1209
www.nathanturner.com

Vessel
114 Kensington Park Road,
London W11 2PW, UK
Tel: +44 (0) 20 7727 8001
www.vesselstore.com

Voon Benson
Unit 3d, Burbage House
83 Curtain Road
London EC2A 3BS, UK
Tel: +44 20 7033 8763
www.voon-benson.com

TABLES AND CHAIRS

Chaplins
477-507 Uxbridge Road
Pinner
Middlesex HA5 4JS, UK
Tel: +44 (0) 20 8421 1779
www.chaplins.co.uk

The Conran Shop
407 E. 59th Street
New York, NY 10022
Tel: 866 755 9079
www.conranusa.com

The Dining Chair Company
4 St Barnabus Street
London SW1V 8PE, UK
Tel: +44 (0) 20 7259 0422
www.diningchair.co.uk

The Dining Room Shop
62-64 Whitehart Lane
Barnes
London SW13 0PZ, UK
Tel: +44 (0) 20 8878 1+44 (0) 20
www.thediningroomshop.co.uk

Grand Illusions
2/4 Crown Road
St Margarets
Twickenham TW1 3EE, UK
Tel: +44 (0) 20 8607 9446
www.grand-illusions.com

Heal's
196 Tottenham Court Road
London W1P 9LD, UK
Tel: +44 (0) 20 7636 1666
www.heals.co.uk

PARTY PLANNERS,
CATERERS AND FLORISTS

John Carter Flowers
Studio C3, The Depot
3 Michael Road
London SW6 2AD
Tel: 020 7731 5146
www.johncarterflowers.com

Admirable Crichton
Unit 5, Camberwell Trading Estate
Denmark Road
London SE5 9LB, UK
Tel: +44 (0) 20 7326 3800
www.admirable-crichton.co.uk

Preston Bailey
147 West 25th Street, 11th Floor
New York, NY 10001
Tel: 212 741 9300
www.prestonbailey.com

Boxy's
Mortelstraat 91
9831 Deurle, Belgium
Tel: +32 9 385 8733
www.boxys.be

Little Venice Cake Company
15 Manchester Mews
London W1U 2DX, UK
Tel: +44 (0) 20 7486 5252
www.lvcc.co.uk

Melt Chocolates
59 Ledbury Road
London W11 2AA, UK
Tel: +44 (0) 20 7727 5030
www.meltchocolates.com

Peggy Porschen Cakes
32 Madison Studios
The Village, 101 Amies Street
London SW11 2JW, UK
Tel: +44 (0) 20 7738 1339
www.peggyporschen.com

Alison Price & Company
Norfolk House, 5a Cranmer Road
London SW9 6EJ, UK
Tel: +44 (0) 20 7840 7640
www.alisonprice.co.uk

Paula Pryke Flowers
The Flower House, Cynthia Street
London N1 9JF, UK
Tel: +44 (0) 20 7837 7336
www.paula-pryke-flowers.com

Wood Brown Florists
11 Culvert Place
Parkfield Trading Estate
London SW11 5BA, UK
Tel: +44 (0) 20 7622 7501

index

Figures in *italics* indicate captions.

acknowledgments

picture credits

1 the Chairman of Thomas Goode's home in London; 2-3 Carolyn Quartermaine's house in the South of France; 4-5 the Chairman of Thomas Goode's home in London; 7 the Chairman of Thomas Goode's home in London; 8-9 Tricia Foley's home on Long Island, tableware by Wedgwood; 10 Diane Fisher-Martinson's home on Long Island; 11 John Saladino's home in California; 12 Meredith Etherington-Smith's London home; 13 Glen Senk & Keith Johnson's apartment in New York; 14 Sally Sirkin Lewis' home in Beverly Hills; 15 Peri Wolfman & Charles Gold's home on Long Island; 16 left Kristof & Stefan Boxy's home in Gent, with tableware by John Pawson; 16 right the Krakoff townhouse in New York; 17 left Voon Wong's home in London; 17 right Nathan Turner's apartment in Beverly Hills; 18 Nicolette Schouten designer, Collection Privée; 19 above left Nicolette Schouten designer, Collection Privée; 19 above right Gilles & Marianne Pellerin architect, Collection Privée; 19 below left Voon Wong's home in London; 19 below right the Chairman of Thomas Goode's home in London; 20 above left the Krakoff townhouse in New York; 20 above right Vicente Wolf's home on Long Island; 20 below left Carolyn Quartermaine's house in the South of France; 20 below right the Chairman of Thomas Goode's home in London; 21 above Nicolette Schouten designer, Collection Privée; 21 below Sally Sirkin Lewis' home in Beverly Hills; 22-23 Peri Wolfman & Charles Gold's home on Long Island; 25 Meredith Etherington-Smith's London home; 26-29 the Chairman of Thomas Goode's home in London; 30-31 Nicolette Schouten designer, Collection Privée; 32-35 Peri Wolfman & Charles Gold's home on Long Island; 36-37 the Krakoff townhouse in New York; 38-41 John Saladino's home in California; 42-45 Carolyn Quartermaine's house in the South of France; 46-49 Diane Fisher-Martinson's home on Long Island; 50-53 Nathan Turner's apartment in Beverly Hills; 54-55 dining room designed by Stephanie Stokes Inc, Interior Design; 56-57 the Chairman of Thomas Goode's home in London; 58-61 Meredith Etherington-Smith's London home; 62-65 Glen Senk & Keith Johnson's apartment in New York; 66-71 Ebba Lopez's house in the South of France; 72-75 Nicolette Schouten designer, Collection Privée; 76-77 Gilles & Marianne Pellerin architect, Collection Privée; 79 Ebba Lopez's house in the South of France; 80 above left Abigail Ahern's London home; 80 above right Vicente Wolf's home on Long Island; 80 below right Kristof & Stefan Boxy's home in Gent, with tableware by John Pawson; 81 Kristof & Stefan Boxy's home in Gent; 82 Carolyn Quartermaine's house in the South of France; 83 François Gilles' London home; 84-85 Voon Wong's home in London; 86 Glen Senk & Keith Johnson's apartment in New York; 87 Gilles & Marianne Pellerin architect, Collection Privée; 88 Ebba Lopez's house in the South of France; 88-89 Abigail Ahern's London home; 90-91 Gilles & Marianne Pellerin architect, Collection Privée; 92 above left and below Tricia Foley's home on Long Island, tableware by Wedgwood; 92 above right Glen Senk & Keith Johnson's apartment in New York: 93 Tricia Foley's home on Long Island, tableware by Wedgwood; 94-95 Louise Nason of Melt's London home; 96 the Chairman of Thomas Goode's home in London; 97 a house in Hampstead; 98 François Gilles' London home; 99 above Ebba Lopez's house in the South of France; 99 below Voon Wong's home in London; 100-101 Kristof & Stefan Boxy's home in Gent, with tableware by John Pawson; 102-103 Vicente Wolf's home on Long Island; 104 above Diane Fisher-Martinson's home on Long Island; 104 below Gilles & Marianne Pellerin architect, Collection Privée; 105-107 Nicolette Schouten designer, Collection Privée; 108 Peri Wolfman & Charles Gold's home on Long Island; 109 Gilles & Marianne Pellerin architect, Collection Privée; 110-113 John Saladino's home in California; 114-115 Alison Price's house in London; 116 above Vicente Wolf's home on Long Island; 116 center & below the Chairman of Thomas Goode's home in London; 117 Vicente Wolf's home on Long Island; 118-119 Preston Bailey's apartment in New York; 121 Nathan Turner's apartment in Beverly Hills; 122 above Sally Sirkin Lewis' home in Beverly Hills; 122 below Agnès Emery's house in Belgium; 123 Peri Wolfman & Charles Gold's home on Long Island; 124-125 Louise Nason of Melt's London home; 126-129 Alison Price's house in London; 130 Meredith Etherington-Smith's London home; 131 the Krakoff townhouse in New York; 132-133 Sally Sirkin Lewis' home in Beverly Hills; 134 above Ebba Lopez's house in the South of France; 134 below Carolyn Quartermaine's house in the South of France; 135 Ebba Lopez's house in the South of France; 136 Nathan Turner's apartment in Beverly Hills; 137 the Chairman of Thomas Goode's home in London; 138-141 Tricia Foley's home on Long Island, tableware by Wedgwood; 142 Agnès Emery's house in Belgium; 143 © David Clerihew/table design The Admirable Crichton; 144-147 a table set by Johnny Roxburgh of The Admirable Crichton at Chiswick House, chef Rolline Frewen, cakes by Peggy Porschen; 148-149 Agnès Emery's house in Belgium; 150-153 Preston Bailey's apartment in New York; 154-155 Diane Fisher-Martinson's home on Long Island; 157 Gilles & Marianne Pellerin architect, Collection Privée; 158 above the Chairman of Thomas Goode's home in London; 158 center dining room designed by Stephanie Stokes Inc, Interior Design; 158 below a house in Hampstead; 159 Nicolette Schouten designer, Collection Privée; 160 Nathan Turner's apartment in Beverly Hills; 161 above Gilles & Marianne Pellerin architect, Collection Privée; 161 center Ebba Lopez's house in the South of France; 161 below Carolyn Quartermaine's house in the South of France; 162 above Diane Fisher-Martinson's home on Long Island; 162 below Ebba Lopez's house in the South of France; 163 above left & below right Diane Fisher-Martinson's home on Long Island; 163 above right Ebba Lopez's house in the South of France; 163 below left the Chairman of Thomas Goode's home in London; 164 Sally Sirkin Lewis' home in Beverly Hills; 165 above François Gilles' London home; 165 center Kristof & Stefan Boxy's home in Gent, with tableware by John Pawson; 165 below Diane Fisher-Martinson's home on Long Island; 166 above dining room designed by Stephanie Stokes Inc, Interior Design; 166 below Kristof & Stefan Boxy's home in Gent, with tableware by Maarten van Severen; 167 above left & below right the Chairman of Thomas Goode's home in London; 167 above right Tricia Foley's home on Long Island, tableware by Wedgwood; 167 below left a house in Hampstead; 168 the Chairman of Thomas Goode's home in London; 169 above Glen Senk & Keith Johnson's apartment in New York; 169 center Diane Fisher-Martinson's home on Long Island; 169 below Meredith Etherington-Smith's London home; 170 above Tricia Foley's home on Long Island, tableware by Wedgwood; 170 below Agnès Emery's house in Belgium; 171 above left John Saladino's home in California; 171 above right Nicolette Schouten designer, Collection Privée; 171 below left a table set by Johnny Roxburgh of The Admirable Crichton at Chiswick House; 171 below right Gilles & Marianne Pellerin architect, Collection Privée; 172 Vicente Wolf's home on Long Island; 173 above Glen Senk & Keith Johnson's apartment in New York; 173 center Louise Nason of Melt's London home; 173 below Voon Wong's home in London; 174 above John Saladino's home in California; 174 below Peri Wolfman & Charles Gold's home on Long Island; 175 Peri Wolfman & Charles Gold's home on Long Island; 176 above Kristof & Stefan Boxy's home in Gent; 176 center Nicolette Schouten designer, Collection Privée; 176 below François Gilles' London home; 177 Diane Fisher-Martinson's home on Long Island: 178 Peri Wolfman & Charles Gold's home on Long Island; 179 above Preston Bailey's apartment in New York; 179 center Gilles & Marianne Pellerin architect, Collection Privée; 179 below a table set by Johnny Roxburgh of The Admirable Crichton at Chiswick House, cakes by Peggy Porschen; 180 above Alison Price's house in London; 180 below Nicolette Schouten designer, Collection Privée; 181 Nathan Turner's apartment in Beverly Hills; 182 the Chairman of Thomas Goode's home in London; 183 above Diane Fisher-Martinson's home on Long Island; 183 center Alison Price's house in London; 183 below François Gilles' London home; 184-185 Nicolette Schouten designer, Collection Privée; 189 Kristof & Stefan Boxy's home in Gent, with tableware by John Pawson.

author's acknowledgments

First of all I would like to thank, so much, all those generous people—both in the United States and Europe—who created such original and beautiful tables for us to photograph and who went to so much trouble and such extraordinary lengths to make the tables so wonderful and us so welcome.

Back home, I would also like to thank very much Salutiferous Simon for both his lovely pictures and perennial geniality, Generous Jacqui for both suggesting and facilitating the whole project, Sagacious Sian for making it all run so smoothly, Matchless Maggie for producing such a good book and Notable Nadine who did all the detective work.